Teaching Students with Dyscalculia

How to teach students with the Specific Learning Disorder dyscalculia.

Dr. Honora Wall, Ed.D.

PolyMath Publishing

403 Chase Street

Osage, IA 50461

ISBN: 978-1-7327601-6-5

Book cover design by The Good Designer

First printing edition 2022

www.educalclearning.com

Table of Contents

Preface

As a child, I was convinced I could never "do" math. Everyone knew it: my parents, my teachers, my friends, and me. I wasn't a "math person". This was fine with me, as I had no intention of *ever* doing math if I could help it. However, at the time, I didn't realize the truth of the saying, "*Mann Tracht, Un Gott Lacht*": man plans, and God laughs. As an adult, I do math all the time. I teach it, I present on it, I study it, I talk about it, and I write about it. My work experience has led me to my life's work, helping people who have the math learning disorder *dyscalculia*. No one is more surprised by this than I am.

If I were to sum up my childhood math experiences, they all boil down to looking at the board and thinking, "*where the heck did the three come from?*" I did well in other classes, but anything with numbers was not my forte. No one could have convinced me that my life's passion, my research, and my teaching gift would lie in mathematics. Many years later, I was an adult going through a divorce when I realized I would have to make peace with numbers so that I could do my taxes and run my finances. I grabbed my son's third grade math textbook and started from scratch, attempting one math problem at a time. There were a lot of tears, especially when I tackled word problems!

There was also a lot of frustration. Much of that frustration came when I would solve a problem and I would think, *well that was easy, so it can't be right*. But I was right! I realized that most of my earlier mistakes in math were so simple, so basic, that they must have been obvious to my teachers. Why had no one said, "Oh, you're doing *this*, when you should be doing *that*." Small corrections could have changed my entire math trajectory. I was angry, and then I was determined. I did not want anyone else to go through the same experiences I did. I became a math teacher.

I do not have dyscalculia. I know this because time, money, and place value make sense to me. I know my basic math facts and I recall formulas, steps, and procedures easily. These are indicators that I had a poor math foundation and low numeracy, rather than a math learning disability. However, in the course of my teaching and tutoring, I have met many students who do have dyscalculia. I've met frustrated and worried parents. I've met dedicated tutors and administrators who questioned why their students kept struggling and nothing seemed to help. I looked for research, materials, or programs, and found little, especially when compared to the amount of research I found on dyslexia. I decided to pursue my doctoral degree in curriculum and instruction, with a focus on dyscalculia. A lifetime of work has led me to write this book. I hope it helps other educators support their students, and together, we can change math for the millions of students struggling with dyscalculia.

Introduction

In the early 1930's, a neuropsychiatrist in Iowa named Dr. Samuel Orton was working with adults who had suffered brain damage. He examined their difficulties with language and realized that many children shared the same language and literacy struggles, even though the children didn't have brain damage. He became intrigued and shifted the focus of his work to studying childhood struggles with language and literacy. Soon, he partnered with Dr. Anna Gillingham, a psychologist and educator whose work focused on the building blocks of reading: phonics, prefixes, suffixes, and decoding words. Together they developed the Orton-Gillingham method of reading intervention, an entirely new way of teaching reading and spelling, and the basis of our modern approach to helping students with dyslexia.

Dyslexia is a Specific Learning Disorder, a lifelong condition that impacts the way we read, interpret, and comprehend text. Thanks to the work of Orton and Gillingham, dyslexia caught the public's attention and the Orton-Gillingham reading program quickly grew in popularity, training thousands of teachers and helping millions of students. By the 1970's, dyslexia had become a household word to describe struggling readers. Today, specialty schools that target dyslexic students can be found in most communities. Training and certification workshops for educators occur year-round. Almost all public schools in the United States have a Literacy Coach, Dyslexia specialist, or in-class Orton-Gillingham reading instruction. Hundreds of thousands of research articles that examine dyslexia have been published.

Where was the concurrent work in the field of math?

Dyscalculia is a Specific Learning Disorder that impacts the ability to *understand, master,* and *recall* math. Sadly, the published research for dyscalculia amounts to one-tenth that for dyslexia, at the time of this books' publication. When it comes to math, too often, teachers and parents say that children just aren't trying hard enough, aren't paying attention, or just aren't good at math. The truth is more nuanced. Every child wants to feel academically successful and empowered. It is our job to find the best ways to reach them, instruct them, support them, and assess them, based on their learning needs. For students with dyscalculia, this work is vital, but can be frustrating. The purpose of this textbook is to help educators better understand their struggling students and help them achieve all they are capable of.

Dyscalculia and dyslexia are only two of the Specific Learning Disorders (SLDs). In the same family, we can find dysgraphia, a condition that impacts handwriting, organizing thoughts, and creating time-or-order driven events (i.e., understanding first, next, last). People with dysgraphia have trouble holding a pencil properly and also have trouble writing essays in a cohesive order. Then, there is dyspraxia, which impacts the ability to plan, organize, and carry out motor skills in a given space; people with dyspraxia are often called clumsy, bumping into things or tripping over their own feet. They tend to be poor drivers, have poor balance, and have difficulty playing sports. Many times, students have a comorbid diagnosis, combining more than one (or even all) of the SLDs with ADD/ADHD, processing disorders, or Autism.

Studying dyscalculia is fascinating and rewarding. Understanding this disorder requires learning about neuroscience, numeracy, cognition, and human development. It also contains an element of mystery and, for future researchers, exciting discoveries. When we discuss dyscalculia, we have more questions than answers. For example, dyscalculia could come from an error in subitization, the ability to mentally estimate how many objects are in a group. Dyscalculia could stem from a coding issue, which occurs when we combine word form, Arabic numerals, and objects into neurological connections. Many times, it involves visual-spatial issues, which impact the way we should introduce vocabulary and diagrams. Dyscalculia erases math information that has already been learned, but we don't know how or why. There's much more we need to learn about dyscalculia. This book combines research and case studies to illustrate dyscalculia and its effects on students of all ages.

A Road Map for this Book

This book is divided into chapters which take the reader from an introduction to dyscalculia, a description of the disorder throughout the K-12 school experience, and a comparison of dyscalculia versus other barriers to math success. Each chapter begins with a brief overview, then takes a deep dive into dyscalculia-specific learning issues. This "deep dive" section shows educators how students with dyscalculia understand math differently. It describes what we know about learning, conceptualizing, remembering, and recalling math information, along with the interventions and accommodations that help these students both learn and demonstrate their knowledge. These ideas can be immediately implemented in any classroom.

Every chapter includes a *Case Study*, a true story of one of my students and their journey from struggling to successful student. All names have been changed to protect their privacy, but the histories, evaluations, struggles, and triumphs are all true. It has been an honor to see so many people overcome their fears of math! I am grateful I was able to be part of these inspiring journeys. Next, *Understand, Master, Recall*, is designed to address the learning needs of students with dyscalculia at various age and grade levels. The final section of each chapter contains a short set of *Exercises* designed to measure the reader's understanding of dyscalculia. Answers are included in the back of the book. The *Endnotes* and *Additional Resources* section at the end of the chapters will lead interested readers to the research foundations of this book and its claims.

Happy reading!

Chapter 1: Dyscalculia

"I believe that the only true education comes through the stimulation of the child's powers by the demands of the social situations in which he finds himself... Through the responses which others make to his own activities he comes to know what these mean in social terms."

-- John Dewey

There is a group of learning disabilities that are tied to neurological development. These Specific Learning Disorders include dyslexia (reading), dysgraphia (handwriting and organization), dyspraxia (movement and balance), and dyscalculia (math). Dyscalculia is a learning disability that affects approximately 10% of the population-- roughly 5 million school age children in 2021-- inhibiting their ability to learn, remember, and recall mathematical information.[1] Although dyscalculia is discussed in medical journals dating to the early 1900's, our understanding of this disorder is quite thin. Dyscalculia involves neurodivergent (atypical) development, brain wiring and coding issues, conceptual struggles, and visual-spatial issues. Luckily, the proper accommodations and interventions are simple and can be implemented in any classroom, using any math curriculum, without a lot of expense. This textbook discusses appropriate age and grade level accommodations and interventions in each chapter. First, let's discuss what we currently know about dyscalculia.

An Overview of Dyscalculia

Dyscalculia, like all SLDs, is a lifelong condition created by neurological differences. People can be born with dyscalculia (called developmental dyscalculia, or DD) or it may result from a brain injury (called acquired dyscalculia, or AD); in both cases, this is a condition that can be accommodated, but not treated.[4] This is an important distinction for educators: we do not teach students with dyscalculia to "get over" their learning difference. We support them throughout their entire education journey, knowing they will always process math in a unique way. We know that children with dyscalculia perform in the lowest-achieving groups in math class, often reporting difficulties knowing how to tell time, understand money, or remember basic math facts.[3] When these three issues, *telling time, working with money,* and *forgetting math facts*, do not improve with practice or remedial instruction, it is a key indicator of dyscalculia.

Dyscalculic students are resistant to many intervention strategies. This is partly due to the nature of the disorder, which involves the degeneration of learned information over time.[6] For example, numeracy includes the ability to visually estimate quantities when looking at a group of dots (called *subitization*).[5] People with dyscalculia do not estimate, they have to count each of the dots, every time, and because of this, they have delayed development of automatic counting methods.[8] Additionally, the Approximate Number System (ANS), an important foundation of all math skills, is weak or underdeveloped in people with dyscalculia.[9] We will discuss these in greater detail in later chapters.

Accommodations such as calculator use, reference sheets, or worked examples are shown to benefit dyscalculic students, but interventions including differentiated instructional strategies only have occasional success. This poor response to interventions versus accommodations is a notable difference between students with a learning disorder and those with a weak math foundation. Children with a weak foundation can receive remediated instruction and move on successfully without support. Children with dyscalculia will always need support, as dyscalculia persists throughout the lifespan.

For educators, perhaps the most frustrating aspect of dyscalculia is the **loss of math information** over time. We don't know why people with dyscalculia forget the math they have already learned; we just know they do. We know that the parietal lobe is where we store math-related knowledge. We know that, for most people with dyscalculia, this region acts more like a colander than a storage bin. Students can answer questions in class, take great notes, complete their homework well… then do poorly on a quiz… then look at a test review as if they have never seen the topic before, then fail the test. It seems that math information drains right out of long-term memory. Some people with dyscalculia lose math information quickly, while some forget over time; some people will benefit from a quick reminder, while some need all of the steps and definitions and worked examples presented again, every time a math concept comes up. This uncontrollable loss is one reason why consistently using support systems is crucial for students with dyscalculia to master math.

There are numerous ways of identifying dyscalculia. The most precise method of diagnosing dyscalculia requires an evaluation conducted by a neurologist or psychologist. A neuropsychological evaluation relies on a battery of tests to screen for either a "discrepancy between performance on mathematics achievement tests and expected performance based on age, intelligence, and years of education" or an "impediment in mathematics, evidencing problems with number sense, memorization of arithmetic facts, accurate and fluent calculation, and accurate math reasoning."[11] These distinctions are important for identifying core deficits and selecting meaningful interventions or accommodations. A diagnosis is given when the student performs at or below the 25th (or sometimes 30th) percentile on the math portion of standardized tests. Some psychologists prefer to diagnose dyscalculia based on a 25th percentile rank or lower, based on the normal bell curve. Many researchers use a 30th percentile cutoff for inclusion in dyscalculia studies. Using either the 25th or 30th percentile rank is more a matter of preference than anything else; the difference between scoring at the 25th or 30th percentile can come from great guesses, or really poor guesses, on three to five evaluation questions.

A second sign of a potential learning disability is a student who performs two grade levels below their peers in math. In early elementary, it can be difficult to determine if a student is truly behind their peers, or if they are simply developing at their own pace. This is one reason why many learning disorders are diagnosed after 3rd grade. A third method of identifying dyscalculia is through state mandated testing: students who score a Level 1 or Level 2 could have dyscalculia, or low numeracy, or test anxiety. This method gives the least amount of information about the underlying reasons why a student has low performance.

Understanding time, working with money, and forgetting math facts

Understanding time, working with money, and forgetting math are three key indicators of dyscalculia. People of all ages with this SLD say they are always late, they can't figure out what time to start getting ready for work or school, and they don't know how to read a clock. Even when they read a digital clock, they might read the numbers they see (say, 7:45), but they won't know if this means they are early, late, or on time. This problem is crippling in early elementary school, where reading a clock and answering elapsed time problems takes prominence. In this way, early elementary school can act as a gatekeeper, placing students on a remedial math track they stay on through middle and high school. Time is also a problem for adults with dyscalculia, who need to arrive to work on time, get to an appointment, or juggle carpooling schedules. In this way, dyscalculia erodes quality of life as well as report card grades.

Using appropriate accommodations during quizzes and tests can help students answer questions about time. These accommodations include alternative assessments that use matching questions rather than fill-in questions (i.e., "Draw a line from the digital clock that says 2:15 and the analog clock that shows 2:15"), letting students use a clock with movable hands as they answer questions, or letting them refer to their notes during a quiz or test. Some teachers worry that support tools like this reduce the validity of assessment results, but appropriate accommodations only level the playing field for students with learning disabilities. They do not give struggling students a benefit over typically developing students.

Working with money is challenging for dyscalculics of all ages. In many ways, the growing popularity of debit cards and online purchases has helped because few people use cash or handle change anymore. Many adults with dyscalculia report feeling embarrassed when people talk about money, and many do not want to self-disclose a learning disability to their peers and employers. For young students who have dyscalculia, the challenges of solving money-related problems makes passing second and third grade difficult, if not impossible. When asked which coin is worth more, a nickel or a dime, these students are likely to choose the nickel because it has a larger diameter. When asked to find the total value of a group of coins, they struggle to remember the value of each coin, and then they struggle to add the total values together. This continues to happen no matter how many times we drill coins, bills, their values, or the rules of adding, because the parietal lobe continues to lose the information once it has been learned.

The good news is that the brain works as an integrated unit, not as separate regions or sides or areas that do not overlap. Teachers can assist all students by using a variety of instructional methods that engage different areas of the brain, but for students with dyscalculia, multimodal instruction is a necessity. Games, projects, activities, and class discussions help students develop more complex *schemas*, which are basically concept clouds of knowledge. For example, when we see the letters C-A-T, we instantaneously think of cats, felines, allergies, kittens, tuna, Halloween, tigers, a cat we had once, or the cat our neighbors had, or the one we wish we had gotten for our birthday, black, calico, gray, tabby, or maybe even the song the Siamese cats sang in that old Disney film. This is a schema, a group of related ideas we have about a topic. The more developed and detailed our schemas are, the more we remember them, and the better we can apply them. Teachers who use a variety of teaching methods help students develop greater schemas. This may increase storage of math knowledge outside of the parietal lobe, making it easier for students with dyscalculia to remember.

Prominent researchers

We know very little about how we learn, comprehend, and remember math, and we know even less about why we *don't*. There are some key researchers who have studied dyscalculia, but their assumptions about the causes of the disorder are widely different. Brain Butterworth's work searches for a core deficiency of dyscalculia, similar to the core deficiency model of dyslexia.[5] Other researchers, like Geary, feel that dyscalculia stems from a coding issue or that the learning disability has multiple sources of deficiencies, like visual-spatial issues and working memory issues.[4] Dehaene, Piazzi, and Cohen use neuroscience to uncover the mental number line that seems to underpin all math knowledge.[13] For people who have dyscalculia, there can be multiple areas of math struggles with great individual differences. Some dyscalculics can remember some math facts, some are good at remembering problem-solving steps, and some can easily extend patterns and rotate shapes, while many are at a loss mastering any these topics. Almost all dyscalculics are forward-moving, linear thinkers who struggle with "backwards" math (subtraction, division, roots, etc). More research needs to be done before definitive answers are found.

From 1930 to 1980, research into dyscalculia was conducted mostly by neuroscientists, not educators, but the struggles of K-12 students with dyscalculia increased interest in the field of education research. Still, the work was slow and the interest in math education was low, as compared to the national interest in improving reading. The exciting work of doctors Orton and Gillingham brought dyslexia to the forefront of education research and reading programs like the Orton-Gillingham, Wilson, and others spread around the world. Today, a Literacy Coach, certified reading professional, or reading intervention program can be found in almost every school in the United States. The same cannot be said for our understanding of how to teach math, especially for struggling students. Myths about gender- or race-based biases regarding mathematical abilities persist. Teachers cling to outdated beliefs about how students can achieve math mastery (hint: it isn't a matter of practice, practice, practice!). These debunked ideas and instructional approaches have stunted many students' growth as mathematicians.

Early dyscalculia research laid the groundwork for our understanding of this disorder, but did not have the benefit of modern medicine and neurodivergence research, which has added greatly to our understanding. Margaret Reinhold of London published a paper on Specific Learning Disorders in 1951 which described the experience of adults with dyscalculia, dyslexia, dysgraphia, and dyspraxia. She noted that dyscalculia includes *asymbolia*, a disconnect between the operational symbols $(+ - \times \div)$ and their meaning (to add, subtract, multiply, or divide).[12] She reported that people with an SLD may have difficulty drawing a clock face or a coordinate grid with proper labels and intervals. In a very informal way, drawing activities like these can act as a classroom screener for learning disabilities: teachers can ask students to take a blank piece of paper and draw a clock, coordinate grid, or other math-related images. The results will give educators a wealth of information about their student's visual-spatial skills.

Neurological framework

Neuroscientists have added a great deal to our understanding of dyscalculia. We know that researchers can use MRI scans to show that the parietal lobe is less engaged during math activities for people with dyscalculia than for people without.[15] We know that learning through memorization activates the language-based left part of the brain while learning through strategies activates the right, visual imagery part of the brain. We know that subtraction, division, and other backward computations require more oxygen (more mental fuel) than forward activities like adding or multiplying. Neurologists have also shown that translating word problems into algebraic equations activates more neurological connections-- meaning it requires more effort-- than looking at an algebraic equation and thinking about how to solve it. However, we do not yet know how to turn these studies into pedagogy, curriculum, or textbooks.

Math, the brain, and human development

Children all over the world develop an understanding of counting objects, the idea of having more or less, and the ability to recognize and extend patterns. This happens naturally, as part of typical human development-- except when it does not. For some children, the parietal lobe develops weakened neurological connections; mathematical thinking develops slowly and with great difficulty.[7] We know that some people are born with this math disability (Developmental Dyscalculia, or DD) or it can be caused by traumatic brain injury (Acquired Dyscalculia, or AD). What we do not know is how dyscalculia causes different ways of thinking, learning, or remembering math, or why it causes people to lose math information over time. Understanding typical math development can help us understand atypical development.

Researchers describe four stages of typical mathematical skill development: **cardinality, comparison, problem solving**, and **measurement**. These skills develop from birth to six years of age, with a normal range of fluctuations (some children will develop skills early, some late, but most will develop their skills in the middle of the age range). First, there is **cardinality**, which develops through the acquisition of number competence: *symbolic* and *non-symbolic estimation*. Non-symbolic estimation happens first. We see this in young children, primates, and other animals who are able to choose between a set with more or fewer objects. People with neurotypical development will choose a set based on the quantity of objects included, regardless of the size of the object or the set (i.e., a circle or square) they are contained in. Children with dyscalculia might choose a set containing fewer objects, if the objects are larger in size, regardless of quantity.

Knowing that one group is larger than another, based on the quantity of objects within the group, is different from knowing that one group contains three objects while another has five objects, which is symbolic estimation. Symbolic estimation means connecting a quantity of objects with a digit or Arabic numeral. Ask a child with neurotypical development to point to a set with three stars, and they will answer quickly and correctly. Ask a child with dyscalculia the same question, and they will pause to count the number of stars in each set before choosing the right one. They will probably count on their fingers.

Another aspect of cardinality is looking at a group of objects and estimating how many objects are in the set, called subitizing (Figure 1). Subitization leads to the automatic processing of quantities—for example, looking at a die and knowing which side has five dots without counting-- and supports addition and subtraction. Subitization is the foundation of grouping, estimating, pattern recognition, and skip counting. People with dyscalculia have a delayed or non-existent automaticity of subitization, which slows down both their work and their understanding of math operations. Subitizing isn't singular to people; it has been seen in monkeys, birds, and even bees.

Figure 1. *Subitization.*

The dot set on the left shows a standard array which most people will automatically count as five dots. The dot set on the right shows how dyscalculics tend to think of all arrays; they will have to count each dot, for every array, including the one on the left.
Image credit © EduCalc Learning 2022

The final aspect of cardinality is developing *Approximate Number Sense* (ANS). Dyscalculia inhibits ANS development. In most cases, we expect to see a well-developed ANS before preschool. Children will learn the number words *one* through *ten* by listening to people count, and making a connection between the letters that form these words, the phonics involved in saying these words, and the quantity of objects they represent happens around four years of age. Rote counting (i.e., saying number words in order, like one, two, three, four, five) happens before children connect a word with a number of objects it means (for example, "three A's" means A, A, A). This one-to-one correspondence (one word matches only one quantity) becomes automatic. Soon children learn to count by 2's, 5's, or 10's, and next they develop the ability to start from any number and count on (i.e., the teacher says 7, and the student says 8, 9, 10). These actions form our Approximate Number Sense, and they are difficult for children with dyscalculia. Having a strong ANS is important because it supports computation, among other skills. Research shows that repeated math practice does not strengthen ANS in students under 12, making it hard for teachers to strengthen ANS in elementary school.

Comparison is the second stage of mathematical development. Comparison is a natural activity that develops automatically. We see it in toddlers, who know when things are similar or not, and they like separating and organizing things. By fourteen to eighteen months of age, children go beyond simply making "same" and "different" judgments. Now they can also tell which group contains more *quantity* than another. Children make these simple comparisons, not by counting, but based on which set looks like it contains more than the other set. Comparison can be skewed if objects are not equally sized but are physically larger or smaller, like comparing a basket of five thin crayons versus a basket of three oversized crayons. The larger-sized crayons can make a basket appear more "full", and therefore greater. Making this mistake is common for young children-- and older dyscalculics—who tend to choose "more" or "greater" based on physical size instead of quantity.

Young children are naturally great at **problem solving**, which is the next stage of mathematical thinking. By five years of age, children can use blocks or drawings to solve simple addition and subtraction problems. In kindergarten and first grade, many children can use concrete materials to act out the actions in problems that involve grouping objects into sets or separating objects into equal piles. This shows that young children understand multiplication and division, even though they do not understand mathematical symbols like 3 x 4 or 15 ÷ 3. Typically developing children may move away from using objects for problem solving well before the end of first grade. For children with low numeracy, using objects to solve problems is a great way to strengthen mathematical thinking and reinforce math facts in both first and second grade. For children with dyscalculia, using objects to solve problems is a great accommodation that could last through third grade, though most children of this age will not want to use objects for problem solving in front of their peers.

The final stage of building mathematical thinking is **measurement**. Concepts like length, weight, and volume develop when children place objects side by side, lift a variety of objects, or pour water from a cup into a bucket or the bathtub. Later, they can reason that if a book is shorter than a string, and the string is shorter than a table, then the book must be shorter than the table. This type of comparison is a far cry from measuring in units like inches or centimeters, but it is the foundation of all measurement. Children need time to master this phase before they move onto things like units, rulers, or conversions, even though most math programs introduce these items too early for typical development. Students with dyscalculia will struggle with the basic concepts of measurement longer than their peers. Older students have the added problem of being confused by multiple counting bases, place value, English customary measurements, and the Metric System. They will benefit from having reference sheets or a set of worked examples whenever they are working on measurement problems. They may need alternative assessments, like talking about measurement rather than completing worksheets, to demonstrate knowledge.

Four stages of math development:

Cardinality: *Non-symbolic and symbolic representations of amounts.*

Comparison: *Deciding between larger and smaller quantities.*

Problem solving: *Building a bridge between the known and the unknown.*

Measurement: *Length, weight, volume, and other descriptions of capacity.*

Case Study 1: Cheryl

When I first met Cheryl, she was entering fourth grade but was stuck doing kindergarten math work. Her school wasn't willing to let her move ahead until she had correctly finished the kindergarten math book. Cheryl was diagnosed with dyslexia and dyscalculia; the teachers and administrative staff at her school understood dyslexia as a reading disability, but they weren't familiar with the term "dyscalculia" at all. Cheryl, her teachers, and her parents were frustrated with Cheryl's inability to do below-grade level work. Her teachers wouldn't give her grade-level work until she could master her original worksheets. She didn't know what she was doing wrong or what to do differently, and felt incapable of ever reaching this goal. Cheryl's parents decided to move her to a small private school that might be better suited to meet her learning needs. The school recommended me as a math specialist who might be able to help.

Cheryl's mom, Cynthia, phoned me to talk about summer tutoring. She didn't know if there was much hope for her daughter. Cheryl already had four years of math struggles behind her, and it seemed she was destined to never understand numbers. The family's goals for Cheryl were to see if she could do any math at all, and to make her school experience more positive. Cynthia and her husband weren't concerned with Cheryl getting to grade level math. Her mom had "never been much of a math person" herself and they didn't want to set unreasonable goals or make Cheryl feel more pressured than she already did. She told me that Cheryl was very shy and not very happy about doing math at all, especially not over the summer. We set a schedule of one-hour sessions, once a week, to see what Cheryl might be capable of.

Cheryl was polite but withdrawn, understandably so. Her lived experiences with math and math teachers were universally negative. She stayed in her room until her mom made her come out. She did not make eye contact with me and didn't have a lot to say. I knew that jumping in with standard math tools-- pencil, paper, worksheets-- would shut her down even further, so I began our work by asking her questions. How did she feel about math? How did she feel about herself as a mathematician? Which math topics did she feel good about, or at least, which ones did she feel the least badly about? For every emotion-based answer she gave ("I hate it", "math makes me sad"), I affirmed her feelings ("I can understand that", "I would probably feel that way too") without attempting to change or challenge what she said. When she talked about her past math experiences in school or at home, I allied with her ("That must have been incredibly frustrating" or "No wonder you didn't want to try after that"), rather than asking her to see things from the adult's point of view. When she talked about math topics that scared her, I was reassuring, instead of contradicting her feelings ("Oh yeah, fractions are the worst. We'll fix that, but not for a while. We have plenty of time before we worry about doing that!"). I've found that this approach is vital for helping struggling students: first, meet them where they are, without judgment. Validate their feelings without asking them to validate anyone else's feelings. Acknowledge their challenges and struggles without making them feel bad for having them. I listen to a lot of teachers and parents who are pretty good at the first half (meet students where they are, validate feelings, acknowledge struggles) but terrible at the second half (without judgment, without disrespecting their feelings, without making the student feel inadequate).

I asked Cheryl to pick one math-related thing that she wanted to talk about. She chose shapes. She felt like she knew what shapes were, but she always got low scores on her work, and she wanted to know why. "Ok," I said, "think of everything you know about shapes, and tell me what you know." She could describe shapes by their names ("Well, there are triangles and squares and circles") but was confused by their design elements (i.e., number of sides). "Ok," I said, "I want you to look around the house and find me examples of all the different shapes you can think of." She came back with a box of cereal and a bowl. We talked about the names for these shapes and how hard it is to find a triangle-shaped item lying around, unless there's a bag of Doritos handy. We decided to make a poster of shapes, and she wanted to put the names of each shape *inside* the shape on the poster, because when she looked at a page filled with objects and words, she wasn't always sure which ones went together. At this point, I learned as much as Cheryl did that day. I realized that she had a disconnect between text, drawings, and objects; they weren't coded together into one concept. Once we identified this disconnect, we made a poster with large shapes so that Cheryl could write the shape name and its characteristics inside the shape itself. We also used colors to tie all important information together. Viola! Cheryl never had a question about shapes again.

Many of Cheryl's math struggles came from this type of disconnect. Once we identified a disconnect we immediately created the necessary connections through discussions, creativity, and real-world objects. Cheryl progressed quickly and we jumped into grade-level math topics, fixing her foundation as we went along. We used support tools-- a calculator, her notes from our sessions—at all times. Cheryl was able to pass fourth grade math and remained on grade level. Five years later, she has become a confident, engaged math student who believes she can learn any math topic. She even ranks math as one of her favorite subjects! Cheryl still uses her calculator and relies heavily on her notes, much in the same way a near-sighted person wears their glasses forever.

Understand, Master, Recall: Birth to Pre-Kindergarten

Human development may be relatively linear, but it is highly individualized. Students with dyscalculia have atypical development. They will move through the same stages of mathematical thinking as other children, but at a slower pace. Since early childhood phases typically last from birth to six years of age, the signs of atypical development may not raise a red flag until a child is in second grade or third grade. Some late-blooming children will catch up with their peers on their own. Some will have low numeracy, math anxiety, or a background of trauma, and they can catch up with their peers through targeted interventions. For some, time and interventions will not make a meaningful difference; this can be a sign of dyscalculia.

Understand.

In every culture, all over the world, humans have developed an understanding of one, two, and three objects. In some communal cultures, amounts greater than three are simply, *more*. This elemental numerical understanding comes from interaction with our environment. For example, as soon as we gain motor control, we start picking things up. We group things together in piles. We move objects from here to there and into and out of containers. Mathematical thinking comes from *interacting* and *doing* something. When we take a group of different objects (some pencils, some blocks, some coins) and we separate them into piles (three pencils, three blocks, three coins), we create a connection between quantity and the word "three". We practice this concept by counting every kind of object we can find: three cars, three carrots, three chairs, three friends, etc. Then we move away from concrete objects and think of "three" as an amount on its own. Later, as we build our mental number line, we recognize "three" as being to the right of zero but to the left of five. We can also compare three as being more than two but less than four, and we can code the phonic sounds of *th*/rē as separate from *tr*/ē. The sound of *tr*/ē can then be coded to an image of an oak, maple, or Blue Spruce. Some researchers feel that dyscalculia could involve a coding issue between amounts, Arabic numerals, and written words (Figure 2).

Figure 2. Coding and numerical cognition

Arabic digit	Word form	Object representation
3	three	O O O

The brain codes numeric information in three ways: The Arabic numeral, the written and spoken word representing the amount, and a concrete, object-based representation of the amount. Researchers question whether dyscalculia stems from an underlying coding issue. ©EduCalc Learning 2021

Master.

Parents and early educators play a key role in developing numeracy beyond one, two, three. It's important for educators to remember that young children learn through play (of course, all children through play, but most schools are ill equipped to support play as an instructional tool for older students). Creating numeracy should be fun! It should be physical, collaborative, and enjoyable. It should be tactile and verbal. Please do not attempt to quiz children in a Head Start program on one-to-one correspondence using worksheets. Instead, just count things throughout the day and throughout the school or playground. Sing counting songs. Point out printed numbers on signs or doorways. Make numeracy a relaxing, natural part of your normal day. Mastery comes from a repetition of enjoyable, successful experiences. Create these events and let mastery develop naturally, over time.

Recall.

At this stage, recall is a premature goal. Instead, this stage is where we lay the groundwork for math knowledge that can be recalled in later years. Young children should be playing games that develop memory skills without the stress of assessing memory. Teachers can build the foundation for future recall by helping children develop deep neurological connections called *schemas*. A basic description of a schema is to think of it like an idea cloud. It's a collection of all the thoughts, experiences, memories, emotions, and understanding we have of a word or concept. Children from birth to 5 years are building their schemas and they need all the help and enrichment they can get. Give them as many chances to build a schema around numbers as you can (and make them fun!).

Well-developed schemas support automaticity. Older students with dyscalculia will need strong math schemas to help them understand and recall math information that the parietal lobe loses. They will need multiple experiences of learning basic math facts, including stories, songs, and pattern recognition, rather than simply working with flash cards. They will need multiple experiences of discussing and identifying cardinality and ordinality, comparing, and estimating, including using objects, creating groups, or drawing pictures. Use real-world events and examples frequently. Dyscalculia cannot be avoided or overcome, nor does it have to be. When students with dyscalculia are supported properly through accommodations and enrichment, they will succeed.

What about worksheets? Some early childhood programs use worksheets to promote handwriting and other skills that will be useful later. However, we learn math (and most everything else) through interacting with our environment, not through simply printing symbols like letters or numbers. Move away from the worksheets and give children objects. Let them count, sort, order, combine, stack, and separate to their heart's content. Counting three blocks today, three dolls tomorrow, and three toy cars the next day builds cardinality. Placing the red block first, the yellow block second, and the green block third builds ordinality. Sorting and combining builds pattern recognition. Showing you their creations builds confidence and self-esteem. Hearing praise for their work creates a definition of self as a mathematician.

Chapter 1 Questions and Exercises

1. People with dyscalculia can get better at math with extra practice. True/False

2. Many people struggle with math because they aren't good students. True/False

3. Dyscalculia affects 8-12% of the population. True/False

4. Three key indicators of dyscalculia include:

    a. Low math scores, poor learning attitude, and working speed.
    b. Trouble telling time and working with money, and forgetting math facts.
    c. Speed, study skills, and telling time.

5. The four stages of early math development are:

    a. Cardinality, comparison, problem solving, and measurement.
    b. Skip counting, comparison, shape sorting, and measurement.
    c. Cardinality, counting principles, problem solving, and work ethic.

6. Where does dyscalculia come from?

    a. Genetics.
    b. Brain injuries.
    c. Both are possible.

7. Which of the following are Specific Learning Disorders?

    a. Dyslexia, ADHD, ELL.
    b. Dyscalculia, dyslexia, dysgraphia.
    c. Any learning challenge.

8. What is subitization?

    a. Automatically estimating amounts.
    b. A form of subtraction.
    c. A type of math instruction.

9. Write a 250-word reflection to the case study. Have you had a similar experience with a student? How would you have approached helping this student?

10. Write a 250-word reflection describing early mathematical skills from birth to five years of age.

Endnotes

[1] Butterworth, B., Varma, S., & Laurillard, D. (2011). Dyscalculia: From brain to education. *Science*, *332*(6033), 1049-1053.

[2] Horowitz, S. H., Rawe, J., & Whittaker, M. C. (2017). The state of learning disabilities: Understanding the 1 in 5. New York: National Center for Learning Disabilities.

[3] Kaufmann, L., Mazzocco, M. M., Dowker, A., von Aster, M., Goebel, S., Grabner, R., & Rubinsten, O. (2013). Dyscalculia from a developmental and differential perspective. *Frontiers in Psychology, 4*, 516.

[4] Geary, D. C. (2011). Consequences, characteristics, and causes of mathematical learning disabilities and persistent low achievement in mathematics. *Journal of Developmental and Behavioral Pediatrics: JDBP, 32*(3), 250.

[5] Butterworth, B. (2005). The development of arithmetical abilities. *Journal of Child Psychiatry* 46, 3–18.

[6] Shalev, R. S., & Gross-Tsur, V. (2001). Developmental dyscalculia. *Pediatric Neurology, 24*(5), 337-342.

[7] Price, G. R., & Ansari, D. (2013). Dyscalculia: Characteristics, causes, and treatments. *Numeracy, 6*(1), 1-16.

[8] Bélanger, P. (2011). Learning theories: Discussion. *Theories in Adult Learning and Education* (49-52).

[9] He, Y., Zhou, X., Shi, D., Song, H., Zhang, H., & Shi, J. (2016). New evidence on causal relationship between Approximate Number System (ANS) acuity and arithmetic ability in elementary-school students: A longitudinal cross-lagged Analysis. *Frontiers in Psychology, 7*, 1052.

[10] Mazzocco, M. M., & Thompson, R. E. (2005). Kindergarten predictors of math learning disability. *Learning Disabilities Research & Practice, 20*(3), 142-155.

[11] American Psychiatric Association. (2013). *Diagnostic and Statistical Manual of Mental Disorders* (5th ed.). Arlington, VA.

[12] Reinhold, M. (1951). Some clinical aspects of human cortical function. *Brain, 74*(4), 399-431.

[13] Dehaene, S. (2011). *The number sense: How the mind creates mathematics*. OUP USA.

[14] Eliez, S., Blasey, C. M., Menon, V., White, C. D., Schmitt, J. E., & Reiss, A. L. (2001). Functional brain imaging study of mathematical reasoning abilities in velocardiofacial syndrome. *Genetics in Medicine, 3*(1), 49-55.

[15] Grabner, R. H., Ansari, D., Reishofer, G., Stern, E., Ebner, F., & Neuper, C. (2007). Individual differences in mathematical competence predict parietal brain activation during mental calculation. *Neuroimage, 38*(2), 346-356.

[16] Cook, B. G. (2001). A comparison of teachers' attitudes toward their included students with mild and severe disabilities. *The Journal of Special Education, 34*(4), 203-213.

[17] Ohio State University. (2019, April 4). A 'million word gap' for children who aren't read to at home: That's how many fewer words some may hear by kindergarten. *ScienceDaily*.

Chapter 2: Dyscalculia in Grades K-2

"Children acquire knowledge through experience in the environment."

-- Maria Montessori

"Infant gardens." That's what kindergarten, a German invention dating to the mid-1800's, used to be called. Today's kindergarten class might more accurately be called "Infant Topiary," where five-year-old children are molded into chair-sitting, worksheet-completing chapter book readers with no behavioral issues. Too often, there's more anxious stress than magical blooming going on, with dire results for growing children. From 2016 to 2022, The Centers for Disease Control reported increased rates of childhood anxiety.[9] The Journal of the American Academy of Pediatrics reports greater rates of Major Depressive Episodes (MDE) in children as young as twelve. After years of being under stress, older children have underdeveloped executive function skills, low self-esteem, poor self-control, self-regulation, and poor coping skills.[9] However, when we relieve stressors and allow kids to be kids in peaceful, joyful experiences, these negative trends can be avoided.

Students with Specific Learning Disorders experience greater amounts of stress and have lower self-esteem than their peers, adding another barrier to academic achievement. A growing body of research shows specific ways stress and anxiety block learning, memory, and recall by putting the brain in survival mode, releasing and inhibiting important chemicals like serotonin and adrenaline.[5] Early childhood educators should watch for signs of stress in the classroom while children are learning and practicing new skills. Tears, stomach aches, obsessive organization, or clenched fists can all be signs of frustration.[9] When young children exhibit signs of stress, back away from rigidity and let them have some fun. Play creates a lovely garden where all children can bloom.

Dyscalculia in Early Education

Between roughly three and seven years old, children pass through five broad stages of understanding math operations: **Emergent, perceptual, figurative, initial,** and **facile.** All children move through each phase depending on their own rate of development, and some children take longer than others to master these skills. Not every child who struggles has dyscalculia, though, making it hard to distinguish slower development from neurodivergence. Mastering these early stages-- *emergent, perceptual, figurative,* and *initial*-- creates the foundation for successfully understanding a formal math curriculum, like the ones used beyond second grade.

Developing Mathematical Competencies

The *emergent* stage begins when children say numbers in order (one, two, three, four, and so on), usually while counting on their fingers or when counting a group of objects. Next, they will connect these words and quantities to Arabic symbols (1, 2, 3, 4, and so on).[7] They are able to point to a written number, like 2, and correctly name it ("two!"). The emergent stage is defined by connecting a number to a quantity, for example, knowing that this many objects * * * matches the word "three" and the Arabic symbol "3". This is called one-to-one correspondence.

One-to-one correspondence is mastered when children can also tell that * * * would not match the word "five" or the Arabic symbol "7". Children with dyscalculia may show difficulty matching a number to a quantity of objects, or they may spend more time physically counting objects long after their peers mentally count a group of objects.[3] Early childhood through second grade teachers should offer as many opportunities to count objects as possible. If children are slow to develop one-to-one correspondence, or if they are slow to count a group of objects mentally, give them concrete objects to work with. Give them extra time to answer questions because they are counting from one, every time, for every problem.

In the *perceptual* stage, children are able to add visible quantities: if they have three blocks and two blocks, they can combine these to five blocks. If they are given a picture of six stars and another picture of one star, they can combine these to a total of seven stars. However, they need a physical representation of quantities in order to add; they are not ready

30

to look at a written number (4) and create a mental image of this quantity (◇◇◇◇).[4, 12] To an adult, they seem like they are adding the same way we do—using a mental number line and an internal algorithm of the addition process-- but they have a limited ability to understand counting when they do not have concrete objects.[11] They may not be ready to add using only written Arabic numerals, even if they seem to be adding fluently. Students with dyscalculia will not develop this fluency, even with repeated practice. This remains true through first, second, and even third grade. Students with dyscalculia rely on immature counting methods longer than their peers.

The *figurative* number stage involves counting each item rather than counting on from a number. For example, a student might be given the problem 3 + 2, and they will hold up three fingers on one hand, saying "one, two, three". Then they will hold up two fingers on the other hand, saying "four, five!". This is a crucial stage of counting and children should not be rushed through this process. Ask any sports coach or music teacher how often they drill the basics, and they will answer, *always*. However, in math, we like to see students move ahead as quickly as possible without revisiting earlier skills. This is a mistake. Students without dyscalculia will soon hold up three fingers, say nothing, and then count on to five. This is because they are building a mental number line they can count with. Students with dyscalculia may never take this step, because they do not develop a mental number line at the same time or in the same way as their peers. Having objects to count, encouraging finger counting, and using a 1 to 100 chart are external number lines which are appropriate accommodations for these students.

Next is the *initial* number stage. Children in the initial stage are able to connect operation symbols like + or - with the concepts of counting more or taking some away.[1] They know that each written number is tied to one specific quantity, meaning the symbol "3" can only match the set ◇◇◇ but not the set ◇◇◇◇◇.[7] However, children with dyscalculia may need to count each diamond in each set before they know which one has 3 and which one has 5. For these children, the initial stage lasts longer than for other children, due to the weaker parietal lobe. At this time, there are no published studies regarding interventions that can strengthen this skill. This is why using appropriate accommodations is crucial for students with dyscalculia, in the same way wearing eyeglasses is appropriate at all times for students with vision problems.

Most children in this phase can easily count both forward from 1 to 5, and backward, from 5 to 1, but this is not true for students with dyscalculia.[11] Most children with dyscalculia find all types of "backward" math more difficult to do, and teachers may see students struggle with counting down from a number, subtracting numbers, and understanding division, even after they master counting on, adding, or multiplying. Again, external support tools like using objects or 1 to 100 charts will help these students complete work properly. Getting the correct answer is a key part of learning material in any class. Students need successful experiences to reflect on before they can create strong neural connections. Being "right" facilitates learning.

Next is the *facile* number stage. It is the final building block of a young child's math foundation. This is the phase where counting strategies become more advanced, basic facts are recalled quickly, and students begin to be labeled as being "good" or "bad" at math.[12] One indicator of the facile number stage is when students use doubles to compute faster: if they are given the math problem 5 + 6, they may strategize that 5 + 5 is 10, and 6 is one more than 5, so the answer must be one more than 10. Students with dyscalculia will not use this doubling strategy during any stage of mathematical or personal development, even in adulthood. In fact, many shortcuts and math tricks are indecipherable for people with dyscalculia. They simply don't make sense, and therefore, they don't help.

Seeing students who are incapable of using these time-saving strategies can be frustrating for educators who are comfortable using shortcuts and mental math tricks. It is important to know that these strategies, while a time saver for you, are the opposite for your students. For instance, if you ask a student to add 7 and 2, a student with well-developed numeracy can answer "seven, eight, nine", because they start at 7 and count on. While the "counting on" strategy works, it requires many neural connections which some students don't have. For them, thinking about the strategy requires *more* mental energy, not less. A struggling student may need to count their fingers, one to seven, then hold up two additional fingers to decide on a total amount; this can be a sign of either low numeracy or dyscalculia.[1] Students with dyscalculia always demonstrate a delayed development of advanced skills.[3]

Some researchers feel that dyscalculia stems from a coding deficiency between Arabic numerals, word form, and quantity. Teachers can use multiple strategies to support coding, and should provide ample opportunities to practice coding. This can come from playing matching games, playing card games, or displaying posters with numbers, words, and images. 1 to 100 charts and number lines should be displayed in the classroom and students should have a copy at their desk. Songs, books, and puzzles that strengthen counting should be incorporated into daily activities. Early elementary educators can use multimodal instruction to enrich development and create a strong math foundation.

Subitization, Cardinality, and ANS in Elementary School

Subitization and cardinality are part of the Approximate Number System (ANS), our mental ability to understand quantity. In very young children, ANS is measured through subitization (matching a set of dots to an Arabic number). Many of us are familiar with sets of dots on dice and playing cards, and automatically know how many dots are in a set (Figure 3). Subitization is the ability to look at the box on the left and know it contains three circles, and that the box on the right contains ten circles. Cardinality is understanding that the written symbol "10" corresponds to the ten circles, the word form "t-e-n", and that the digit 10 applies to 10 circles, or 10 apples, or 10 horses, or any group of 10 objects. Children with dyscalculia do not develop subitization and may struggle with cardinality. In later years, subitization remains weak, and dyscalculics often report continuing to count on their fingers and needing more time to think about objects, amounts, and numbers well into adulthood.

Figure 3. *Subitization and cardinality.*

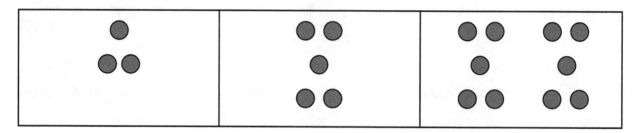

Subitization is the ability to glance at the boxes and know that the box on the left contains three dots while the box on the right has ten dots. Cardinality is the understanding that the number "5" describes only the amount held in the middle box, but not the amount held in the other two boxes. These two skills are the foundation of the Approximate Number System.
© EduCalc Learning 2021

We can test ANS development by showing students two groups of dots and asking which set "is bigger".[6] Students with dyscalculia struggle with this task, as they usually choose the set of dots with a bigger diameter, or the set whose dots are spread out to take up more space, rather than comparing the number of dots in each set.[3] As our ANS becomes stronger and more automatic, it takes less time to look at the first set in Figure 3 and think "3" or the last set and think "10". This automaticity helps us estimate amounts, understand place value and grouping, and compare amounts. It also helps us work faster, using less mental energy. However, students with dyscalculia will count each dot, in each set, every time. They may never develop automaticity; therefore, they always work harder and use more mental energy than their peers.

At this time, we don't know enough about how the Approximate Number System is developed or how to strengthen it in students who have learning disabilities. We know that ANS is key to automatic math computation.[6] We know that repeated math practice does not strengthen the ANS in children under twelve.[6] We know that people with dyscalculia have a lesser developed ANS, even as adults.[6] For these reasons, playing games or leading students in activities for ANS development will help most students, but those with dyscalculia may never develop the same automaticity as their peers. That's ok; learning disorders like dyscalculia are not problems we need to fix. They are neurological differences that we should address. Offering students with dyscalculia the appropriate support during all math activities is the best way to increase their math mastery. This support comes from using 1-100 charts, using a number line, using counters or other manipulatives, or using a calculator.

Not all difficulties are signs of a learning disorder. Dyscalculia is present from birth, but usually not identified before third grade or so. This is partly due to the wide range of ages when kids reach developmental stages; for example, counting accurately from 1 to 10 can happen anywhere from four years old to six years old, and an intervention program could help a slower learner master this skill. We begin to think about possible learning disabilities when applied interventions don't make a difference. Students who are simply learning at their own pace will show improvement, usually permanent, after receiving interventions and extra help. Students who *do* have dyscalculia will continue to struggle with things like counting, counting on from any number, and adding, even after repeated interventions.[3] They won't develop automaticity or number fluency. Flash cards won't help. Extra homework won't help. However, using a number line or 1-100 chart during classwork, homework, quizzes, and tests *will* help. Educators should know that using support systems takes more time and effort than working fluently. Using appropriate accommodations does not inflate performance. Using accommodations will not make assignments inherently easier for students, they just make the work manageable.

Case Study 2: Ernesto

Ernesto was a student in my first-grade class; his brother Miguel was in kindergarten, but doing first grade level work, so they were frequently together. Luckily they got along very well, and Miguel was a comfort to Ernesto, who frequently became anxious and nervous in class. As the year progressed, though, Ernesto became aware that Miguel caught on faster; his younger brother could read more words fluently, he could add and subtract faster with fewer mistakes, and he could answer more questions quickly. Ernesto spent more time in small group instruction or one-on-one remedial sessions to improve his reading and mathematical skills. Ernesto's parents were not interested in having him tested for learning disorders because they didn't want him to be "labeled" or to "feel different". The irony is that Ernesto *already* felt different, but without testing, he didn't understand why.

I suspect Ernesto has dyscalculia because he never became comfortable with numbers, even when using a 1 to 100 chart or number line. He approached them as if he were seeing them for the first time, every time. He never grew to enjoy math class. When he would add, his answers were often within a digit or two of being correct. He would add 6 + 4 to 9 or 11, instead of 10. Using a 1 to 100 chart helped him, but only when he used proper finger placement. On days when he was tired, grumpy, or frustrated, he moved his fingers along the chart smoothly, without counting each square. I learned to watch for his emotional state and prompt him to place a finger on each square individually as he counted. In hindsight, I could have given him a token or plastic coin to move from square to square as he counted. I don't know for certain if this would have helped him count with precision, but as teachers, part of our job is to experiment until we find a useful tool to support our students. For teachers who have students with dyscalculia, this trial-and-error process continues long after other students have developed age appropriate, reliable counting methods on their own.

By the end of the year, Ernesto had made little progress in math. His work lacked mastery, which is important to building a strong math foundation. He had few successful math experiences to reflect on. I let his parents know my concerns, and told them that, when a student remains stuck or frustrated working with smaller numbers, this may be a sign that further diagnostic testing is called for. They resisted further testing, which was their right. I continued to offer Ernesto extra support by encouraging him to use 1 to 100 charts, prompting him to work with accuracy, and assigning fewer problems at a time.

I wish I could report on Ernesto's mathematical competencies today, but the family changed schools and I have not heard from them. Teachers have one school year– 180 short days– to make the most impact we can before our students leave our classroom. Ernesto and Miguel left not only my room, but also the school, as the family moved into a new district. Classroom teachers rarely hear about a student's future successes or struggles, and this was true for me in Ernesto's case. I hope his future teachers noticed that his struggles were not typical, and that they were able to continue giving him the interventions and accommodations that would help him progress through school.

Understand, Master, Recall: Kindergarten to 2nd Grade

Early elementary is a time of new beginnings and foundation building. No teacher or parent expects to see a learning disorder in very young children, and we like to give students time to catch up to each other before we label anyone as having a serious barrier to learning. However, the signs of dyscalculia are evident in very young children. Teachers who know what to look for can offer enrichment and interventions that can prepare students with dyscalculia to do their best in the coming years.

Understand.

Perhaps the most important thing to understand about elementary math students is that they are doing *children's math*, not adult math, even though these two things look the same to an outside observer. We can hand an addition worksheet to a second grader, a fourth grader, and a college student, and watch each of them write down their answers. Visually, it seems that they are all doing the same thing: adding. In reality, the college student is most likely retrieving memorized facts without pondering quantities or total sets in any way.[13] The second grader could be either explicitly counting discrete objects (like their fingers) or imagining pictures of distinct objects as they count in their heads.[6] The fourth grader's comprehension and work could be anywhere in between.[7] It is important to avoid assumptions about what children *know* based on what they are *doing*, because we can't tell which cognitive processes are in motion just by watching students do work.[1] Ask younger students to tell you how they got their answer, and praise their methods. Model other methods they might try. Make note of their preferred methods and tailor support systems to meet their needs and abilities.

Master.

The best way to master counting is to count! Everyone in the classroom should be counting, all the time. Be sure to model counting on a daily basis.[12] Teachers, assistants, administrators, and visitors can all count items in the classroom, and the number of visitors can be counted by students. In kindergarten and first grade classrooms, hold up items as you count them. Point to a class poster of word form numbers as you count and hold an object. Be sure to make a mistake sometimes– say "1, 2, 3, 5… Oops! I forgot the four!" then correct yourself. It is important for students to see you make mistakes and it's important for them to see how you *acknowledge* and *recover* from them. Modeling is always more effective than simply telling.

In a perfect world, all classrooms in every grade would use game play to reinforce learning, including middle and high school classes. At the very least, early education should include as much playtime as possible.[12] Matching games can help children code numbers, word form, and quantity.[1] Sorting objects and describing their differences and similarities (by number of objects, color, or shape) helps students develop cardinality.[6] Teachers should reinforce concrete counting methods and not be fooled by a student who appears to be using more advanced counting, adding, or subtracting methods. Children develop skills across a wide range of time; building a strong foundation early is the best way to ensure future math competencies.

Recall.

We recall information that has been previously moved from working memory (also called short-term memory) to long-term memory. Working memory is like the on ramp to a highway: fast, brief, easily congested, and the only way to get onto the highway. In early education, the working memory on-ramp leads to literacy and numeracy.[10] Multiple research studies show that working memory skills are important for both reading and math. In fact, working memory skills in 5- and 6-year-olds are indicators not only of current math ability, but also predictors of future math achievement.[2] One study found that working memory was a better predictor of math performance than either verbal or performance IQ.[10] This shows the importance of playing memory games in early elementary school. Kindergarten, first, and second grade students should be strengthening their memory skills daily, through play.

Working memory is easily affected by stress. When we are under stress, our short-term memory holds less information, loses information quickly, and sends less information back to our long-term memory.[9] Stress can come from school, from home, from the community, or from environmental causes. Many times, we have no idea what kinds of current or background stress our students are dealing with. For students with dyscalculia, math class creates stress on an almost daily basis. Teachers who want to ensure success should incorporate social-emotional learning strategies as frequently as possible. Following Social-Emotional Learning principles supports all students, especially those with a trauma background or current stressors in their lives, and can support memory development as well.

Social-emotional principles reduce stress by helping students manage their emotions, their friendships, and their reactions to the world around them. Social-emotional strategies in the classroom can come from district-wide initiatives, or they can be as simple as having regular class discussions. Talk to young students about the many ways they can solve problems; talk about the resources available to them, like asking a teacher, a friend, reading a book, or following an example. Play games that are interactive, collaborative, and easy for all students to feel successful in. Model making mistakes and recovering from them. Model asking questions. When classrooms feel safe, the work we do feels manageable, and this leads to better learning.

What about technology? I saw a post in an online forum for math teachers where a kindergarten teacher asked for referrals of a computer-based math program for their students. In kindergarten. I was saddened by the question and by the number of responses offering technology as a key piece of early elementary math experiences. We know that technology acts more as a dopamine trigger than a learning tool. It reinforces the idea that correct answers, and therefore learning, should be tied to external rewards like bells, badges, or electronic confetti. This reinforces external motivation and undermines internal motivation. Technology can also mask a lack of understanding when the user just clicks things until they get a reward stimulus. We have no idea if the student comprehends the information or if they can apply it to future problems. Technology can be a great tool in later years, but its use in early elementary classrooms should be limited.

Chapter 2 Questions and Exercises

1. Children develop mathematical thinking over many years. True/False

2. Practicing math on worksheets strengthens the ANS in young children. True/False

3. Children with dyscalculia struggle to develop automaticity when counting. True/False

4. The five stages of mathematical thinking are:

    a. Emerging, practicing, mastering, showing, and teaching.

    b. Concrete, abstract, manipulative, figurative, and written.

    c. Emergent, perceptual, figurative, initial, and facile.

5. Subitization helps people:

    a. Mentally estimate and compare amounts.

    b. Subtract math problems.

    c. Substitute values in math problems.

6. The Approximate Number System (ANS) includes:

    a. Subitization
    b. Cardinality
    c. Both are part of ANS

7. Coding math concepts includes:

    a. Matching quantity, words, and images in our heads.
    b. Matching two or more ideas in our head.
    c. The cardinality and ordinality of numbers.

8. Working memory:

    a. Is something everyone has in equal amounts.
    b. Is negatively impacted by stress, but can predict later math achievements.
    c. Develops naturally over time and has little impact on learning.

9. Write a 250-word reflection to the case study. Have you had a similar experience with a student? How would you have approached helping this student?

10. Write a 2-3 page paper describing an intervention lesson to boost one of the following skills: subitization, numeracy skills, or coding.

Endnotes

[1] Dept. of Education and Training. (2003). *Developing efficient numeracy strategies.*

[2] De Smedt, B., Janssen, R., Bouwens, K., Verschaffel, L., Boets, B., & Ghesquière, P. (2009). Working memory and individual differences in mathematics achievement: A longitudinal study from first grade to second grade. *Journal of experimental child psychology, 103*(2), 186-201.

[3] Dowker, A. (2005). Early identification and intervention for students with mathematics difficulties. *Journal of learning disabilities, 38*(4), 324-332.

[4] Fanari, R., Meloni, C., & Massidda, D. (2018). Visuospatial working memory and early math skills in first grade children. *International Association for Development of the Information Society.*

[5] Fyfe, E. R., McNeil, N. M., Son, J. Y., & Goldstone, R. L. (2014). Concreteness fading in mathematics and science instruction: A systematic review. *Educational psychology review, 26*(1), 9-25.

[6] Gebuis, T., & Van Der Smagt, M. J. (2011). False approximations of the approximate number system. *PloS one, 6*(10), e25405.

[7] Hahkioniemi, M. (2004). Perceptual and symbolic representations as a starting point of the acquisition of the derivative. *International Group for the Psychology of Mathematics Education.*

[8] Laski, E. V., Casey, B. M., Yu, Q., Dulaney, A., Heyman, M., & Dearing, E. (2013). Spatial skills as a predictor of first grade girls' use of higher-level arithmetic strategies. *Learning and Individual Differences, 23*, 123-130.

[9] Luethi, M., Meier, B., & Sandi, C. (2009). Stress effects on working memory, explicit memory, and implicit memory for neutral and emotional stimuli in healthy men. *Frontiers in behavioral neuroscience, 2*, 5.

[10] Nevo, E., & Breznitz, Z. (2013). The development of working memory from kindergarten to first grade in children with different decoding skills. *Journal of experimental child psychology, 114*(2), 217-228.

[11] Osborne, A. R. (1973). Perceptual burdens in learning mathematics. *The Arithmetic Teacher, 20*(8), 626-629.

[12] Passolunghi, M. C., Mammarella, I. C., & Altoè, G. (2008). Cognitive abilities as precursors of the early acquisition of mathematical skills during first through second grades. *Developmental neuropsychology, 33*(3), 229-250.

[13] Steffe, L. P. (2004). PSSM from a constructivist perspective. *Engaging young children in mathematics: Standards for early childhood mathematics education*, 221-251.

Chapter 3: Dyscalculia in Grades 3-5

"I have no special talent. I am only passionately curious."

-- Albert Einstein

Children are naturally, passionately curious. Sadly, many children with dyscalculia have lost their natural curiosity about numbers before they leave elementary school, after repeated failures, embarrassments, and indignities. Children with dyscalculia face years of negativity and become adults with diminished self-confidence who are shut out of many careers and have lower earning potential.[6] This path begins in early elementary school. It is firmly set before middle school. Much of this trajectory is caused by elementary school math topics. Math classes in grades 3 through 5 place a heavy emphasis on the four operations (adding, subtracting, multiplying, and dividing). Students are expected to master these operations using integers, decimals, and fractions, both through computation and word problems. For students whose parietal lobe erases both basic math facts and problem-solving procedures, these topics can be highly difficult to master. Students who receive very poor grades in elementary math may be placed on lower-level or remedial math tracks.[6] They start Algebra later, take math courses that may not meet graduation requirements, and are unprepared for college entrance exams. They earn less than their adult peers without dyscalculia.[6] The lifetime earning potential for people with dyscalculia can be predicted from their elementary school experiences.[6] Elementary educators have the power to change this through understanding the dyscalculic brain.

Time, Money, and Place Value: The Dyscalculia Trifecta

Perhaps the worst math topics for people with dyscalculia are the "Dyscalculia Trifecta": *time, money, and place value*. These topics are introduced in early childhood education and continue through fifth or sixth grade. Then they are never heard of again! No one in Pre-Calculus is making change from a ten-dollar bill. The Dyscalculia Trifecta introduces a wide variety of counting bases. Place value changes for every ten units. Telling time changes in at least seven different ways: clocks use 60 minutes, 12 hours, halves, and quarters; calendars use 12 months, 4 weeks, 7 days (5 for a "work week"). Money varies by coins and bills and the ways to make a dollar or how to make change. Students with dyscalculia would like us to pick a base and stick with it!

Having the right support tools is crucial to learning the Dyscalculia Trifecta. Support tools should be easy to read, not visually complex or overwhelming.[12] Examples include clock manipulatives with moving hands, a 1-to-100 chart for counting, and a reference sheet with pictures of coins or bills and their values. These tools are appropriate for classwork, homework, quizzes, and tests. They provide external structure for people whose parietal lobe does not develop a strong, automatic, internal structure through the ANS. Be aware that older students will not use tools designed for younger children, especially in front of their peers. It is embarrassing to be the only student with a bright yellow clock on their desk. Manipulatives must offer the right kind of topic support, and be age appropriate as well.

Time

Telling **time** plagues people with dyscalculia their whole lives. Time involves hours, minutes, seconds, days, weeks, months, and years, all of which have a unique base system for counting (except for minutes and seconds, which both use base 60). Reading analog clocks requires knowing which hand points to minutes and which hand points to hours; which one is written first-- hours before minutes, unless you're saying "quarter till" or "quarter after" or "half-past"—and thinking about noon versus midnight. The ideas of daytime and nighttime, which are broken down again into morning, afternoon, and evening, are hard to apply to a clock face. Applying elapsed time to activities is difficult not only for people with dyscalculia, but also those with executive function issues or ADHD. Adults with dyscalculia say they are always late or early, and feel nervous about taking too long or not having enough time. For people with dyscalculia, time remains a jumbled mess of confusion.

One intervention that can help students understand elapsed time is a work clock (Figure 5). A work clock uses color to signal the beginning and end of an activity. Prompt students to think of elapsed time by stating the activity while referencing the work clock: "You have 20 minutes to work on your classwork. When the minute hand gets to 12:15, the black line, I will let you know you have five minutes left. When the minute hand gets to 12:20, the red line, we will turn in classwork and get ready for recess." When students look at the classroom clock and compare its hands to the work clock, they have a concrete demonstration of the abstract idea of passing time. Labeling the work clock hands reinforces coding as well.

Figure 5. *Work clock.*

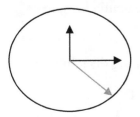

A work clock uses color to show when activities begin and end. This visual signal demonstrates elapsed time. It should look like the wall clock in your classroom. For example, do not use a work clock with Roman Numerals if your wall clock uses Arabic numbers.
© EduCalc Learning 2022

Money

For students with dyscalculia, learning about **money** poses multiple problems. There are different counting bases (1 dollar, 4 quarters, 100 pennies, etc.), different visual cues to recognize and decode (images of bills and coins versus decimals versus word problems), different computations to perform (adding and subtracting), and different procedures to follow. When the parietal lobe stores procedures like items in a kitchen junk drawer, it is difficult to know where to start. For instance, the rules for adding and subtracting decimals are different than the rules for multiplying or dividing decimals, but they both need to be used when working with money. Students with dyscalculia also forget their basic math facts and may have visual-spatial difficulties.[4] This impacts both their working speed and their ability to line up decimals properly before adding or subtracting them.[11]

Remember that students with dyscalculia are likely to believe that a nickel has more value than a dime, due to its larger diameter. Students should have a reference sheet with images of coins and their values. Teach students to verify their work by using the reference sheet to identify values, using their 1 to 100 chart or number line for adding and subtracting, and using graph paper to write problems vertically, organized by the decimal point. Require that all students attend to precision, which ensures more right answers. Right answers equate to more successful experiences to reflect on, which builds stronger neural networks.

Working with money is challenging for dyscalculics of all ages. Adults with dyscalculia shy away from situations where they may be asked to make change for customers, or careers where they need to track finances. People with dyscalculia learn to avoid embarrassment by avoiding money altogether. Many adults report feeling embarrassed when people talk about money, and they are scared to self-disclose a learning disability to their peers and employers. This limits their future jobs and lifetime earnings. When dyscalculics of all ages feel comfortable using the right support tools to handle money with confidence, they can increase their self-confidence and change their future.

Place Value

Blame it on Aryabhata, a mathematician in 5th century India. He invented place value for Hindu-Arabic number systems. Place value is a way of demonstrating quantity through position. For example, in the number 5,432 we know that the digit 5 has a value of 5,000 because of its *placement* in the string of numbers.[9] In other number systems, large quantities are shown with special characters, rather than a specific position: the Egyptians and Romans did not use place value at all.[9] Look at the comparison of three different number systems in Figure 6, which show three different civilizations and the ways they demonstrate quantity.

Figure 6. *Representing quantities through symbols.*

Roman	Chinese	Arabic
LXXII	七十二	72
50 + 10 + 10 + 1 + 1	Seven "tens" and two	70 + 2

The symbols used to represent quantities may, or may not, incorporate place value.

Aryabhata was ahead of his time– place value was in use 100 years before the concept of zero was developed. This early development doesn't help people with dyscalculia, though, who struggle with all aspects of place value. Understanding place value is believed to be a function of working memory and visual-spatial skills, which may or may not be strengthened by working with manipulatives.[9] This area of domain-specific knowledge in children with learning disabilities needs more research; we know very little about *how* struggling students understand time, money, or place value, and less about *why* these deficiencies exist or *what* should be done to support these students.

Studies suggest that students with learning disorders can represent quantities and place value through manipulatives, but cannot match their work with the written digit problems in a textbook or on a worksheet.[12] The concept taught by place value blocks does not automatically transfer as knowledge that applies to a worksheet or textbook. There seems to be a limited ability to create a bridge between these pieces of information. Whenever possible, give students alternative assessments, like verbal assessments, in addition to or instead of written ones. They are likely to perform better when they demonstrate or explain place value in their words, using their own tools.

Back-and-Forth Mathematics

Math is full of back-and-forth topics and inverse operations. Adding and subtracting, multiplying and dividing, exponents and roots, theorems and their converses, FOILing and factoring all demonstrate this concept. Typically developing students can master both forward and backward math easily, as demonstrated by "fact family" problems. Students with low numeracy or a weak math foundation may struggle with fact families, but once they reach mastery, they have mastery over both the forward and backward operations. Students with dyscalculia have a much harder time with the "backward" part of math, even once they master the "forward" part. Assessing math in one direction at a time, for example, giving a quiz on addition fact families separate from subtraction, allows students to demonstrate their knowledge rather than demonstrating their learning disorder. Educators may expect that an understanding of the forward part of a concept (for example, multiplication) will automatically create a connection with the backward part (division). Connections like this do not develop automatically for students with dyscalculia. On their own, they do not build a bridge between forward and backward math concepts. Educators need to spend more time building connections with their dyscalculic students.

Seasoned math teachers can teach concepts too quickly because they are so familiar with the questions and the facts needed to solve them. It can be hard to put ourselves in the place of a young child learning about math operations for the first time. For students, math topics are much more complex than they seem to a seasoned teacher. One elementary school example is in teaching decimals. The first hurdle is understanding that decimals represent a quantity between zero and one, and that quantity can become smaller and smaller the more digits there are– even though a long list of digits can look like a "bigger" number, due to its length.[7, 13] Next, we introduce the operations: sometimes decimals need to be lined up vertically, according to the decimal point. Sometimes we have to add zeros as place holders before we can add or subtract correctly. Sometimes we ignore the decimal point, lining up right-justified digits so we can multiply them, and arbitrarily (or so it seems to the student) replacing the decimal point after we multiply. Then we might move all the decimal points before we divide! Under the best of circumstances, working with decimals is a mess. For children with a math learning disability, the mess never gets cleaned up in their mind.

Teachers need to separate operations, rules, and procedures as much as possible, if students are going to have a chance at reaching mastery. Think of the way most math programs teach converting between mixed numbers and improper fractions: if the problem begins with a mixed number, the procedure is to multiply and add. If the problem starts with an improper fraction, the procedure is to divide and subtract. In both cases, the denominator stays the same. Typically developing students will hold different procedures in their mind and choose the right procedure based on the problem they see. Students with dyscalculia aren't sure what kind of problem they are starting with. They aren't sure which procedure matches a given problem. They freeze during classwork and tests, unable to remember how to start. They can benefit from notes with worked examples that help them match procedures to problems. They can also benefit from assessments that clearly separate all problems that begin with a mixed number from all problems that begin with an improper fraction.

Steps and Procedures

Remembering steps and procedures is a stumbling block for students with dyscalculia. Their parietal lobe stores mathematical formulas, operations, and rules like a kitchen junk drawer: too many things tossed into a pile without organization. This is evident when students forget to line up decimals before adding them, or when they confuse the operation needed for perimeter versus area. It is glaringly obvious when these students learn long division. In long division, we repeat the same steps over and over again until we reach zero, or a remainder, or a requested number of digits after a decimal point. Students with dyscalculia seem to forget the third step in long division *even after they have successfully done the same step twice already*. Teachers can prime the class by asking procedural questions like, *What's the first step? What's the next step? What should we do now?* and require that students refer to their list of steps when answering.

Sometimes general education teachers can feel overwhelmed when they think of addressing children with different needs in their classroom. The good news is that one set of accommodations can work well for students with a variety of learning challenges. Students with dyscalculia, dysgraphia, executive function disorders, and ADHD all report confusion in remembering steps and procedures. Students with processing speed disorders need extra time to retrieve this information and perform the work. Students may know the steps but think of them in the wrong order or forget the ones in the middle. They seem to fizzle out halfway through a long problem. Each of these students benefit from the same accommodations: extended time, worked examples, calculator use. Many educators ask if using worked examples, calculators, and the like will give an unfair advantage to some students. The answer is, ***not at all.*** Research studies show that using appropriate accommodations does not inflate academic performance above a student's natural level.

Visual-spatial issues

Visual-spatial skills govern our understanding of location, distance, size, movement, and comparison. They are responsible for developing a mental image of the number line, which supports Approximate Number Sense and mathematical ability.[2] People with dyscalculia have varying levels of visual-spatial skills, but almost all have weakened skills compared to their non-dyscalculic peers.[5] Visual-spatial skills support cardinality and ordinality, too, which explains why these fundamental concepts are poorly understood by older dyscalculic children whose peers mastered these concepts in first and second grade.[5] For instance, most of us rarely think about what is involved when mentally rotating an object, but this is an advanced skill (Figure 7). Most of us master this skill so early in life that we don't have to think about the process anymore; it feels natural because it is automatic. Young children develop this ability through tactile events. They take an object, like a rectangular prism, and rotate it in their hands. They understand that the object remains the same, regardless of whether the shorter end is horizontal or vertical.[10] This is a concrete understanding of rotation. Later, they can rotate an object in their mind, retaining the overall shape of the object as it moves.[14] For kindergarteners, this concrete understanding is tied to mathematical thinking in the parietal lobe. By sixth grade, students no longer need to hold or think of an object; they use visual-spatial memories to *imagine* a rotating object.[10] The rotation process is tied to memory, specifically, visuospatial working memory and visuomotor integration.[2]

Figure 7. *Mentally rotating objects.*

Rotating an object begins as a concrete task, then becomes a mental image of the task; later, students recall a memory of rotation rather than thinking of the task or object itself.
© EduCalc Learning 2022

Students are asked to describe rotation mathematically beginning in third grade.[11] Many students with dyscalculia find themselves stuck as their brains struggle to make the leap from concrete object manipulation to visuospatial memories.[14] Again, this is an area in which building a mental bridge from one activity (holding the object) to another (remembering holding an object) does not happen on its own. Interventions include using concrete objects for practice, during class discussions, or as an assist during assessments.[10] Talk about rotation using one vertex as a reference point (Figure 8). Mark the reference vertex with color, or circling it, or using an arrow to mark the reference point vertex. Model the language you want students to use, i.e.., *"I'm going to look at this point on the top right. See how this point on the top right is sticking out, before the next line points in, to the middle? Ok, when I rotate the shape 90 degrees to the right, that's clockwise, where does that point move to? After the rotation, it points down, to the bottom of the paper."*

Figure 8. *Explaining rotation through marked vertices.*

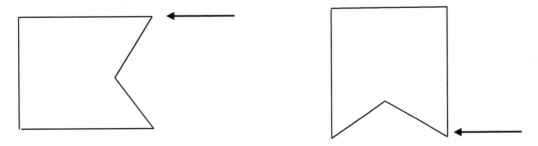

Use arrows, color, or other indicators to mark a reference point for students to focus on. Use specific language to help students code rotation properly. © EduCalc Learning 2022

Case Study 3: Rose

By fifth grade, Rose was very far behind her peers academically. She knew she needed to leave school and try learning from home. Her academic struggles had eroded her self-esteem and made going to school a misery. She was a bright girl with a diagnosis of dyslexia and dyscalculia, but the help she received at school wasn't helping her achieve grade level success. Rose's parents tried using flash cards, completing extra practice problems, buying manipulatives, and watching math instruction videos, all without success. She found a wonderful reading tutor trained in the Wilson reading method, but she wasn't as lucky finding a math tutor. Her dyslexia tutor recommended me for math help. In our first session, Rose hardly spoke at all. Her mother said the family was tired of "fighting about math all the time", and they were hoping to find someone who could handle the math portion of Rose's homeschool curriculum. They weren't hoping for a miracle, just for some peace.

Rose believed this was her fault because she was sure that she was unable to "do math". In her mind, math would always mean failure. She connected math with tears and shame. She was embarrassed by her failures. Rose needed a pathway to success, and she couldn't find one through worksheets and timed tests. The key for Rose was making math accessible through art. She was a very talented artist and would naturally turn a number into a doodle of an animal, an object, or other fun creature. I used this doodling interest as a homework assignment: I had her turn the numbers 1 - 10 into doodles of some kind. Rose took this a step further, saying, "I could make a flip book and each page would have a number with some kind of picture around it," which I happily agreed to. Now she was thinking about Arabic numerals as having some kind of personality, back story, or imagery. She had a math homework assignment that she was excited about; she couldn't wait to start! I had given her a basic guideline (draw numbers with pictures) and she was extending the assignment herself ("I can make a flip book"). This assignment gave Rose a starting point of success that we could build on over time. She knew she could get an A on this assignment, which is a crucial part of reframing negative experiences.

Throughout the year, I would ask Rose what art projects she was currently doing (whether it was drawing, photography, or mixed media pieces, she always had an art project in mind). We added math elements to each of the art pieces she worked on, and soon she was thinking of creative ways to add art into our math topics as well. Before long, Rose was asking for art-based assignments (meaning she was asking for extra math homework!). "I never knew that math was involved in art or music or things like that," she told me. "I thought math was only memorizing numbers and that was it." What a sad statement! Math is so much more than digits and four operations.

Rose's mother reported that, not only were there no more family arguments about math, but also Rose happily talked about the projects she was doing and explained how they related to math concepts. She looked forward to our tutoring sessions and began to ask for more challenging work and independent assignments. This is a sign of confidence and mastery, and is the goal of all scaffolding: to reach the point where the student pulls away from the teacher and wants to work alone. Once this happens, academic growth is fast and furious!

I worked with Rose for two years. By the time of our last session, she was eager to return to a brick-and-mortar school. She looked forward to taking Algebra 1 in 8th grade. When she met her new math teacher, she was able to explain her learning disability and describe the support tools that worked best for her as a math student. Two months into the school year, I received this message from Rose's mother: "Just wanted you to see how all your help with Rose is paying off!" with a snapshot of her math grade: 94% average in the class, including A's and B's on her chapter tests! This kind of success story happens frequently for students with dyscalculia once they understand which support tools they need, know how to use them, and find an avenue for success they can build on.

Understand, Master, Recall: 3rd-5th Grades

Many scholars have criticized the "mile wide and inch deep" math curriculum in the United States. This issue is never more clear than in late elementary school. Our third through fifth grade students are expected to learn basic facts with whole numbers, decimals, fractions, percents, long division, time, money, place value, word problems, measurements in both U.S. standard and metric systems, probability, geometric shapes, equivalent fractions, simplifying fractions, proportions, and more, all in 180 days! We rush students through topics and wonder why students have weak math foundations and poor problem-solving skills. Students with dyscalculia can get lost in the whirlwind.

Understand.

If you've ever taken on a home improvement project by yourself, you've likely noticed that it takes much longer to finish projects on your own than it would if you had hired a professional. Someone with experience and know-how seems to fly through framing a door while the rest of us are still reading the directions. This is because the professional already knows the steps and the process needed to get the job done. The same thing happens with our students; once they understand the steps and process, they can finish their work faster. When we see students in third grade and beyond counting on their fingers, we worry. Why haven't they moved on from that counting method? Why aren't they doing the counting in their head? Actually, these students are counting in two places: with their fingers *and* in their heads.[4] They are reading the instructions while hanging the door.

Finger counting is a tactile activity that builds neural networks and supports all mathematical computations.[11] Some students build these networks quickly. Some students, especially those with a learning disability, need more time to build their networks.[9] People with dyscalculia may never build a strong enough network to support mental counting, as their ANS remains weaker than neurotypical learners.[2] Students who do not have a learning disability will improve their mental counting skills through games, activities, or flashcards. Students who continue to rely on finger counting are displaying greater needs than practice alone can address. In fact, repeated practice has been proven to not help students with dyscalculia in any way. If you use interventions and find they aren't helping, understand that it is time to use external support tools. Do not continue to give students remedial work or extra practice without giving them the tools they need to succeed.

Master.

If a student cannot master memorizing basic facts, is all hope of math mastery lost? No, not at all. In fact, these students have a unique and complex way of understanding math. They reject easy explanations and rules without context. They seek a deeper understanding and look for conceptual development through experiences rather than rote memorization. It can be frustrating for teachers when they are called on to find a new way of explaining concepts, but our old instructional methods will not work here! Our students with dyscalculia require more from us as educators. Their mastery will come from our flexibility.

Instead of expecting students to master memorization, require them to master *confirmation.* Do not accept work until they have used their tools to verify their answers. During class work or intervention periods, have students demonstrate using their tools to find their answers ("*Bill, check your times tables list and tell me what 8 times 7 equals*"). This way, you will teach them not only math, but also the importance of checking their answers and verifying their assumptions.[3] You will teach them how to support themselves as students who will not be held back by their learning differences. You will see far greater improvement in their mathematical understanding and their academic performance.

Another reason why teachers should require that students use a 1 to 100 chart, times tables list, or calculator to check their work is that immediate confirmation strengthens neural networks. The process of predicting and confirming is a key element of increasing or weakening neural connections, and happens automatically, without our realizing it.[3] Class time should include a period of reflection that confirms answers and strengthens connections. In addition, the brain pays the most attention to events that happen at the beginning of an event (primacy) and the end (recency).[3] If the class ends with best-guess work being handed in, this recency period is wasted. If your classroom or tutoring session does not actively support the increase of neural networks, it allows their decrease. You can maximize the recency period by ending each class giving students a few minutes to check their work.

Recall.

Why do students with dyscalculia struggle to recall math information they've learned? Partly, this is due to the parietal lobe losing math information over time.[12] Partly, this is due to prospective memory. Prospective memory refers to our ability to "remember to remember" what we are supposed to be doing.[1] An example of prospective memory is recalling that we need to get milk while we are at the store, or remembering that we need to grab an umbrella if it looks like it might rain. This type of memory is impaired in children with executive function issues, ADHD, dyscalculia, and in older people who have Alzheimer's disease.[1]

We can support prospective memory by reducing the amount of mental energy needed for a task.[1] Break down long problems into smaller steps. Prompt students to think about one step at a time, before having them complete the entire problem on their own (*"Yes, to find the area, we're going to multiply base times height. What is the base here? What is the height? What answer do you get when you multiply them? Great, so what is the area then?"*). Students with dyscalculia can benefit from hearing other students explain how they reached an answer. They can correct themselves as they work through a problem. All this reduces cognitive load and can increase memory acquisition.

What about state testing? Many teachers and administrators worry over student performance on state mandated tests, especially if their state does not allow accommodations during testing. Without accommodations, it is common to see students perform poorly on state tests compared to their performance in class. We would expect decreased performance from a student who wasn't allowed to wear their glasses during a test, too. This simply demonstrates they have an issue that requires accommodations. Focus on increasing comprehension and class academic achievement rather than on testing. Many times, students improve their standardized test performance after using their appropriate support tools during the rest of the school year.

Chapter 3 Questions and Exercises

1. Having a list of steps or procedures gives students an unfair advantage over peers. True/False

2. Mentally rotating objects begins with physically rotating objects. True/False

3. Signs of dyscalculia usually appear later, after 5th grade. True/False

4. Three common math struggles for dyscalculics in early elementary are:

    a. Writing numbers backwards, telling time, and numbers in word form.

    b. Telling time, working with money, and place value.

    c. Completing work, writing numbers backward, and counting to 5.

5. Finger counting after second grade is:

    a. A potential sign of a learning disability.

    b. An example of lazy work.

    c. A crutch that should be discouraged.

6. Students should do grade level work:

    a. After they have mastered the foundations of earlier work.

    b. When they are ready to do the work independent of support tools.

    c. At all times.

7. Forgetting steps and procedures is:

    a. A sign that the student did not study.

    b. Common among people with dyscalculia.

    c. A barrier that cannot be overcome.

8. Place value was developed:

    a. By mathematicians in Babylonia in the 12th century.

    b. By a mathematician in India in the 5th century.

    c. By Renaissance mathematicians in Italy.

9. Write a 250-word reflection to the case study. Have you had a similar experience with a student? How would you have approached helping this student?

10. Write a 3-5 page paper describing how prospective memory, math facts, and procedural memory are used to support or inhibit academic achievement.

Endnotes

[1] Alotaibi, R. M., & Ali, K. J. (2021). Prospective memory in students with learning disabilities. *Specijalna edukacija i rehabilitacija*, *20*(3), 161-169.

[2] Butterworth, B. (1999). A head for figures. *Science*, *284*(5416), 928-929.

[3] Castel, A. D. (2008). Metacognition and learning about primacy and recency effects in free recall: The utilization of intrinsic and extrinsic cues when making judgments of learning. *Memory & Cognition*, *36*(2), 429-437.

[4] Crollen, V., & Noël, M. P. (2015). The role of fingers in the development of counting and arithmetic skills. *Acta Psychologica*, *156*, 37-44.

[5] Dumontheil, I. (2014). Development of abstract thinking during childhood and adolescence: The role of rostrolateral prefrontal cortex. *Developmental cognitive neuroscience*, *10*, 57-76.

[6] Fias, W., Menon, V., & Szucs, D. (2013). Multiple components of developmental dyscalculia. *Trends in neuroscience and education*, *2*(2), 43-47.

[7] Gorev, P. M., et al. (2018). Puzzles as a didactic tool for development of mathematical abilities of junior schoolchildren in basic and additional mathematical education. *EURASIA Journal of Mathematics, Science and Technology Education*, *14*(10).

[8] Kaufmann, L., & von Aster, M. (2012). The diagnosis and management of dyscalculia. *Deutsches Ärzteblatt International*, *109*(45), 767.

[9] Lafay, A., Osana, H. P., & Levin, J. R. (2022). Does Conceptual Transparency in Manipulatives Afford Place-Value Understanding in Children at Risk for Mathematics Learning Disabilities?. *Learning Disability Quarterly*, 07319487221124088.

[10] Mammarella, I. C., Caviola, S., Giofrè, D., & Szűcs, D. (2018). The underlying structure of visuospatial working memory in children with mathematical learning disability. *British Journal of Developmental Psychology*, *36*(2), 220-235.

[11] Moeller, K., Fischer, U., Link, T., Wasner, M., Huber, S., Cress, U., & Nuerk, H. C. (2012). Learning and development of embodied numerosity. *Cognitive processing*, *13*(1), 271-274.

[12] Rapin, I. (2016). Dyscalculia and the calculating brain. *Pediatric neurology*, *61*, 11-20.

[13] Soylu, F., Lester Jr, F. K., & Newman, S. D. (2018). You can count on your fingers: The role of fingers in early mathematical development. *Journal of Numerical Cognition*, *4*(1), 107-135.

[14] Young, C. J., Levine, S. C., & Mix, K. S. (2018). The connection between spatial and mathematical ability across development. *Frontiers in psychology*, *9*, 755.

Chapter 4: Dyscalculia in Grades 6-8

"I cannot emphasize enough the importance of a good teacher."

-- Temple Grandin

No discussion of middle school is complete without a discussion of human development. An incredible number of changes occur between ages eleven and fourteen: growth spurts, emotional regulation, long-term thinking, and abstract thinking are just a few. Middle school teachers manage students displaying the beginning, middle, and end of these changes, all at once, in one classroom. Students with dyscalculia move through the same stages, but need more time to master mathematical concepts than their peers. They tend to be linear thinkers who take longer to understand how to work with variables, solve logic problems, and solve for the unknown.

Measuring Mathematical Growth

How do you know when students are mastering fractions? Researchers look for students who have a "one-half advantage," meaning they can successfully recognize and work with one-half problems (½ + ½) faster and more accurately than problems using other denominators, like one-third or one-fifth.[5] As teachers, we may assume that one-half advantage would happen immediately since these problems are "easy," but we have to remember that nothing about fractions seems easy to students learning about them for the first time. It is a point of success when students can add one-half plus one-half, and another point of success when they can do it quickly. Speed comes from repeated success. More speed and accuracy in this area shows true understanding, rather than great guessing skills, and creates a foundation for working with different denominators.

Examining student knowledge of fractions is important because understanding fractions is a better predictor of future math success than knowing whole-number basic facts.[5] Students *without* dyscalculia gain a one-half advantage in fourth grade. Students *with* dyscalculia may develop a one-half advantage in seventh grade, but only when using visual models.[5] At any grade level, when students with dyscalculia solve fraction problems using only Arabic numbers (as opposed to using models), they show no one-half advantage.[5] This may come from a disconnect between relating what a fraction means (a part of one whole unit) with the visual symbols of a ratio (number over number). For students with dyscalculia, numbers are just written symbols that do not necessarily connect to concepts like quantity, part of a whole, part of one hundred, or the probability of an event.

Our goal in elementary school is to teach the rules of combining and separating while using basic facts to add, subtract, multiply, and divide. Then, in grades 6 to 8, fraction problems shift away from this focus. Middle school problems involving fractions focus on distributive property, solving proportions, and solving algebraic equations.[2] Our goal now is to teach equivalency and inverse operations. Struggling students need the support of a times tables list or calculator to look up basic facts while they learn how to solve these new types of problems (Figure 9). When we deny support, we ask students to do double the work of their peers who have stronger ANS and memory skills.[10] Without the right support, mastery is unattainable.

Figure 9. *Times tables chart versus times tables list.*

x	2	3	4
2	4	6	8
3	6	9	12
4	8	12	16

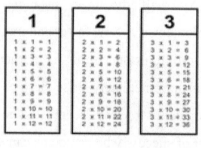

A multiplication chart (left) can be visually overwhelming and confusing to read. A list of the times tables (right) is easier to read and understand. Using a list allows students to find multiples, factors, LCM, GCF, and helps to simplify fractions. © EduCalc Learning 2022

The Right Support: Calculators, Worked Examples, Times Tables List

The great irony of math instruction in the United States is our obsessive relationship with the calculator. First, we refuse to consider the calculator as a legitimate math tool. One can practically hear elementary and early middle school teachers screaming, *"The calculators are lava!,"* followed by a chorus of accusations like, *"You shouldn't have to use a calculator, you have a brain"* or popular lies such as, *"You can't use calculators in (high school/ college/ at your job)"* or *"You won't always have a calculator with you, you need to know how to do it on your own."* Then, students enter Algebra 1. Not only are calculators required, but they must also be an expensive calculator with many bells, whistles, graphing capabilities, and function keys that require an inch-thick manual for proper use. Teachers, it is time to make peace with the calculator. It is a tool, nothing more, nothing less. Using a calculator during classwork, homework, quizzes, and tests is an appropriate accommodation for those with dyscalculia. For these students, using a calculator in math class is the same as letting a student wear glasses when they read. We know that dyscalculia causes the parietal lobe to lose math information over time, and we know that memorizing basic facts is not an appropriate goal for these students. Therefore, using a calculator reduces errors, reduces time spent completing work, and reduces holding children back to below-grade level math work.

Reducing errors counts for much more than just getting the right answer; reducing errors is a key feature of learning. In fact, John Dewey felt learning could not happen without it. When he said in 1933, "We do not learn from experience, we learn from *reflecting* on experience", he was more right than he realized. Neuroscience has caught up to Dewey and we now know that the brain is in a constant state of prediction and either confirmation or rejection.[1] For every piece of sensory input we receive, the brain predicts what will happen next.[7] This is how we add meaning to experiences. When our predictions are right, our brain strengthens those neural networks, and when our predictions are wrong, we do not strengthen those networks.[7] This happens on a level so fast and so subconscious that we are not aware of it (but we can see it on MRIs).[1] For students with dyscalculia, who have experienced years of repeated failures and repeated confusion, the neural networks related to math are weak. Teachers can help strengthen neural networks across the brain by creating, ensuring, and recognizing success as frequently as possible. Calculators help make this happen.

Remember that every calculator is different. Simply handing a student a calculator and assuming they know how to use it is a waste of a reasonable accommodation. Some calculators have a button to square a number, some have a button to take a number to any power, and some have no capability to compute exponents. Some can find square roots, while others find cube roots, any roots, or no roots at all. Some have a button to input negative signs. Sometimes this button is marked with parentheses (-), sometimes with a change indicator (+/-), and sometimes the button doesn't exist. Students need training in order to use their calculator properly. For example, ask students to find the square root of 16 by using their calculators. If anyone gets an error message or no answer, instruction should stop until you have helped them figure out how to get the right answer. Depending on their calculator, they might need to type 16, then press the root symbol, or they might need to reverse that order. They might not have a root symbol and they will need to use a list of perfect squares. Once everyone successfully finds the square root of 16, then the class can move on to solving for other square roots.

Using a calculator is beneficial for a number of reasons. First, using a calculator stops students from falling behind in their workload. Second, it conserves more mental energy, which frees up working memory. Third, it gives students time to reflect on new concepts rather than spending all their time looking up basic facts. For example, think about teaching a unit on finding the area of a triangle. The important part of the unit is learning how to work through the formula and recognizing when to apply it (for triangles, not rectangles, squares, or circles). The extension of the unit is working backward from a given area to find the missing base or height. Nothing about this unit involves learning *how to divide by two*, but this is a key part of the area of a triangle formula. Students with dyscalculia can become stuck on the division and therefore lose all the rest of the lesson. They spend so much time trying to remember their basic facts that they run out of time to finish all the given practice problems. Their answers are usually wrong, and they have nothing to reflect on. The lesson is not learned.

Reducing time wasted on below-grade level work is important at all grades, however, in middle school it takes on more importance than in elementary or high school. This is due to the separation that happens in middle school: students are placed into remedial, average, or

66

advanced academic tracks which are nearly impossible to get out of. In high school, students are placed into classes based on the tracks they were put on during middle school. Many times, students with dyscalculia move onto a remedial track because they are expected to master work below their grade level before they are allowed to move on to the next topic. This is wrong. Once a student with dyscalculia is given the right accommodations, they are perfectly capable of mastering grade level work. Their learning disorder does not need to act as a barrier. They should not be held back by environmental barriers, either.

Graphing, Problem Solving, and Formulas

Elementary school graphing focuses on data: reading and creating pictographs, bar graphs, and line graphs. Middle school graphing rarely touches on these (except for that one chapter near the end of the textbook that covers statistics and probability). In grades 6 through 8, the focus turns to graphing linear equations and all that comes with it: slope, intercepts, functions, and transformations. For all students, graphing successfully requires using symbols correctly, understanding formulas, and developing algebraic insights.[4] For students with dyscalculia, graphing can be difficult due to visual-spatial issues, making procedural mistakes, or struggling with their self-limiting beliefs.[6] They can improve their graphing skills through graphing by hand on a coordinate grid, while using a calculator to complete a table of values. They should have worked examples to follow when moving between standard and slope-intercept form.[4]

Identifying key features of graphs is an important part of algebraic reasoning. Algebraic reasoning helps us compare y-intercepts or describe differences in slope between graphs, and tie these concepts to equations. For students with visual-spatial issues, it can be difficult to match the key features with their spot on a graphed line.[11] Dyscalculia makes it difficult to transfer these concepts onto linear equations as well. Teachers need to spend more time reinforcing coding between looking at a graph, looking at an equation, and performing the math operations within an equation that creates the graphed line. Using color makes a world of difference for students who struggle in these areas. Do not assume that everyone in class is looking at the same axis or interval when you say, "the y-intercept is…", instead, use color to highlight the place you are speaking of. Use different colors for the x- and y-axes, the intercepts, and the graphed line. Use one color to write dashed lines demonstrating slope on the graph, and the same color to write the slope in the linear equation. This support helps the brain connect mathematical operations, visual images, and written symbols.

Students also need to connect graphing with problem solving when they use a table of values or move between standard and slope-intercept form.[6] Many modern math textbooks and programs spend too little time on these concepts, but students with dyscalculia need extra time during assignments to solve these problems, and extra time spent on the concept before moving on. When students have to rush to keep up with a pacing chart, they cannot develop mastery or confidence. Support their efforts by allowing a calculator to solve all problems, during classwork, homework, quizzes, and tests. Give them worked examples to follow, at all times, as well. Worked examples are the math equivalent of labeling folders, drawers, or cubbies. They act as an organization tool for students with dyscalculia.[10] Help students reflect on their mistakes during classwork and have them add these to their personalized notes (i.e., "you did everything right until you had a negative sign" or "remember to start with the intercept first"). Allow them to use these notes, either during quizzes and tests, or at least to verify their work before handing in a quiz or test. Encouraging accuracy and precision increases both success and overall understanding of the concepts.

Problem solving with equations can be difficult for students with dyscalculia because it requires "backward" math. Problem solving is more involved, and more difficult, than solving an equation by substitution (Figure 10). When we know the value of a variable, we can substitute the number for the letter and follow the order of operations given, and find the answer. When we are trying to find the value of a variable, we have to work backwards, like untangling a knot. Students without dyscalculia will start to follow problem-solving steps automatically, with practice. Students with dyscalculia will think about each step in solving a problem, with little automaticity, even after practice. They may need an external reminder, like reviewing their notes before beginning (or while completing) classwork, or a verbal prompt ("*We're going to solve problems by combining like terms. Like terms have the same letter or exponent, and we're going to add or subtract those before we do anything else.*"). Adding in prompts at the start of every class and encouraging students to check their notes can be the only interventions needed to help students solve problem successfully.

Figure 10. *Substitution versus solving equations.*

3x + 5 when x = 2	Substitute 2 for x and solve, using PEMDAS: 3(2) + 5. Multiply then add.
3x + 5 = 17	Subtract 5 from both sides of the equal sign, recognizing like terms (5 does not subtract from 3x). Analyze the next line, 3x = 12. Divide 3 from both sides of the equal sign, do not divide "3x" from both sides.

Solving equations requires thinking backwards from the answer (17) and isolating the variable (x) through inverse operations. © *EduCalc Learning 2022*

Equations and formulas help us solve for any unknown, in any situation, because they give us a set of steps to follow without question. They both use symbolic representations that can be applied to any problem. However, dyscalculia causes the steps and procedures of math formulas to seem like a jumbled mess.[3] This makes equations and formulas a source of frustration rather than inspiration. Without accommodations, students with dyscalculia will solve equations or use formulas appropriately in class and fairly well while doing homework, but not as well on a quiz and may hardly pass a test. This is due to the parietal lobe storing math information incorrectly. Worked examples, a reference list of formulas and which problems they apply to, and notes that remind students how to begin are all appropriate accommodations for dyscalculia.

Some teachers worry that a worked example gives too much information and therefore gives students the answer. In fact, the opposite is true. Students who struggle with mathematical competence, much less mastery, do not have enough knowledge to recognize what to do and when to do it.[7] When we develop a comprehensive set of examples, experiences, and neurological connections to work with automaticity, we have created a *schema*– a set of knowledge that guides actions.[7] Schemas are important because they reduce cognitive load. They free up working memory so we can focus on things like class instruction, looking up basic facts, and performing operations that lead to a correct answer. Having worked examples acts as an external schema by guiding a student's actions, and strengthening their neurological connections.[7] Worked examples do not give an answer any more than a map causes arrival at a destination. The person reading the map still has to move before they can get anywhere.

Formula reference sheets act as external reminders for students without dyscalculia, prompting them what to do to solve a problem. The same is not true for students with dyscalculia. They may have difficulty looking at a formula and matching it to a certain problem. Seeing a formula may not trigger the thought, *"Oh, I need to substitute the four for the r,"* as it would for a neurotypical student (Figure 11). Teachers can create this prompt through modeling: write the formula, then substitute values, then perform the problem-solving operations.

Figure 11. *Formulas should trigger substitution.*

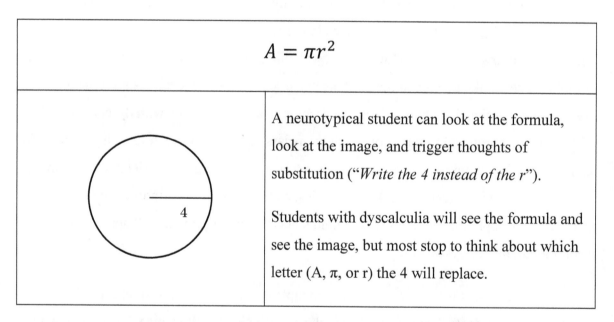

$A = \pi r^2$	
(circle with radius labeled 4)	A neurotypical student can look at the formula, look at the image, and trigger thoughts of substitution (*"Write the 4 instead of the r"*). Students with dyscalculia will see the formula and see the image, but most stop to think about which letter (A, π, or r) the 4 will replace.

On their own, formulas may not support students with dyscalculia. They need worked examples to replace the automatic thought process that other students experience when they work with a formula. © EduCalc Learning 2022

Case Study 4: Kerry

Kerry was diagnosed with dyscalculia as a 4th grade student attending public school in the Midwest. Her mom, a teacher in the same school district, had never heard of dyscalculia. Neither had Kerry's teachers. Neither had a series of tutors who hadn't had success helping Kerry understand or master math. Unfortunately, this is common. Many teachers and tutors understand math very well and are excellent at supporting students with temporary struggles like low numeracy or a weak math foundation. However, few general education teachers or tutors have training in any learning disability, fewer still have heard of dyscalculia, and only a small percentage of those have the right training to address this math learning disorder. For students like Kerry, this means years of falling behind in math, losing confidence in themselves, and solidifying their belief that they just "can't do math".

This continued until Kerry's 7th grade year, when her mom found me in a support group for people with dyscalculia. My first tutoring session with Kerry was online, as we lived in different states. Her mom joined us for the first session (and quite a few after that) and did most of the talking. I spent a lot of that first session answering questions Kerry had about dyscalculia. Was it real? *Yes.* Would she grow out of it? *No.* Was she cheating if she used a calculator? *Not at all.* In my experience, students with dyscalculia need to develop trust when they first reach out for help, more so than most struggling students. They feel ashamed and embarrassed of their math abilities, and they are used to other people making them feel even worse. They expect to be judged. They may develop anxiety and shut down during math-related conversations. Their self-esteem and self-confidence are low. They want to feel understood. We must help these students feel comfortable and accepted before we can help them.

Kerry enjoyed working with shapes and patterns. She liked to work through logic puzzles. She asked lots of questions and she liked to take detailed notes. She was happy at her school and wanted to stay in her math class; this meant our sessions had to cover how to complete her current work, how to explain foundation concepts she didn't know, and how to take notes that could help her in future classes or during quizzes and tests. We didn't go back to work on math concepts from previous years, but we did talk about her math foundation while discussing her classwork. Kerry demonstrated another common trait I have found in most of my students who have SLD's: she had a burning desire to *understand*. Simply giving her a procedure or a formula to follow wasn't enough. She needed to wrestle with the concept before she could move on to the next problem. This is a great quality in a student, but it takes a lot of time to talk out concepts, which most classroom teachers simply don't have. Longer conversations are more appropriate for tutoring or small group sessions.

Kerry was a fast learner and made great progress through tutoring. Over time, we found that her strengths were visual-spatial (graphs, patterns, and shapes) and paying attention to details. A weakness for her was her math-related memory. She used her notes frequently, saying, "Wait, I think I know what this is" and then scanning her math notebook for guidance. Over time, we devised a system of labeling note pages by topic, formula, or outcomes, so she could find the right page later. She had ongoing difficulties with low self-confidence and self-efficacy (our belief in our ability to be successful). She was afraid to answer questions because she was sure she would be wrong. Kerry frequently said, "I'm probably wrong, I don't know, but…". I encouraged her to guess, to talk out her thoughts about how she might solve a problem, and always reinforced her effort (and doubly reinforced her successes!). Finding the right methods for Kerry to learn math took time and effort but was worth it. Kerry was able to stay on grade level math work throughout middle and high school.

Understand, Master, Recall: 6th-8th Grades

Dyscalculia can be differentiated from low numeracy by sixth grade, even by untrained observers (neuropsychological testing can identify dyscalculia much earlier). Dyscalculia presents itself through continued problems telling time or recalling basic facts, continued reliance on counting on fingers or counting from one, and a history of interventions and extra practice that have not helped. Dyscalculia is commonly mistaken for low numeracy, though, especially when students do not have access to professional testing and diagnosis. Many popular programs like Response to Intervention (RTI) or Multi-Tier Systems of Support (MTSS) use ongoing interventions rather than testing to support struggling students. When students continue to move through interventions without being tested for learning disorders, they miss out on the issue-specific accommodations that would truly support their individual needs.

Understand.

When we understand the needs of students with dyscalculia, we can offer the right support. Students with dyscalculia do not benefit from repeating elementary math skills; middle school students need to complete middle school math. Working on grade level is *always* appropriate. Allow students to use calculators and refer to worked examples, as they need external support to replace their underdeveloped ANS. Keep in mind that students can improve their math skills but still say things like, "Wait, did we do this Tuesday?" or "What's 5 times 3? Uh, 16?" This is normal. Dyscalculia causes people to forget what they've just learned or confuse their basic facts.[3] Teach students to verify the formula they need to use, check their reference sheet, and confirm their answers. These actions lead to mastery and self-efficacy. They also lead to better recall, as students use more than just their parietal lobe to store math knowledge. They also develop memories through experiences, events, and emotions.

Master.

Students with dyscalculia need to store math-related information in many areas of the brain, not just the parietal lobe. They can do this by building a strong schema about different math topics, math facts, and processes and procedures. A strong schema looks like this: you walk into your kitchen to start a pot of coffee. You know where the coffee pot is, you know where the filters are, you don't count the steps to the faucet or dig in a drawer to find the scooper. The moment you wake up, your brain fires all coffee-related neurons at once: the smell, the taste, the location of the machines and ingredients, even memories of the best and worst cups of coffee you ever made. You don't need to consciously think about what you are doing. But what happens when you visit family for the holidays? You bang open all the cabinets looking for the coffee, fingers crossed that it isn't whole beans; you turn around twice looking for the sink; you question if you've put enough or too many grounds in the basket; you have no idea if this coffee will be weak, strong, or just right. This is a weak schema because you are in an environment that makes you question everything you do.

You created a strong schema in your own kitchen by doing the same things, with the same tools, with successful outcomes, in a variety of different settings: alone, with friends or family, in summer and winter, early mornings, rushing out the door, and on lazy Sundays. It is vital that students develop a strong schema in math. Teachers can help them develop a strong schema through a mix of class discussions, assigning real-world projects, playing games, writing examples, and ensuring that students are successful in some area. First, success helps students define themselves as mathematical thinkers. Second, success is tied to developing a positive concept of self, which is a key part of a healthy adolescence. Third, the brain strengthens neurological connections that lead to successful outcomes while connections that lead to unsuccessful outcomes waste away. Finally, success increases schema development. With a strong schema, students with dyscalculia have more opportunities to master math topics by recalling more math information.

Recall.

Before we can recall information, we have to store it somewhere. People with dyscalculia have a hard time recalling and storing math information, partly because their working memory skills tend to be lower than for those without dyscalculia.[8] For example, people with dyscalculia have a hard time remembering a set of numbers correctly or saying a string of digits backward. Both of these are signs of working memory and executive function issues. They also predict our mental math abilities. In fact, the better a person is at reciting a string of numbers backward, the better they will do on a math test.[8] Since dyscalculia causes difficulties in storage and recall of math information, educators need to strengthen memory, storage, and recall through activities like creating posters and playing games. Games should be tactile and interactive.[9] One example is a game called "*To the left*", which is played with a deck of cards. Players take a card and can move to the left, or hold their card towards the left, if space or mobility are issues. Students move when you say things like, "Prime numbers to the left." Players with a 2, 3, 5, or 7 move to the left side of the room, while composite numbers move to the right. You can remove face cards or assign them a value. Aces are worth 1, so any player with an ace would stay in the middle of the room. This game can be played using prime and composite numbers, multiples or factors of a number, odd and even numbers, or anything else related to math.

In addition to building memory and math skills, there is an important social-emotional component to having students play games: most struggling students don't get to do it. Typically, playing games, doing coloring or activity sheets, and other fun events are reserved for the students who finish their work before class is done. Students with dyscalculia need more time to finish work, so they miss out on the extras and the "fun stuff" in math class. For struggling students, it confirms their belief that they are not as good as other students. They rarely equate math class with positive experiences and become disengaged from math, both as a subject and as a class.

What about manipulatives? Many students find that using manipulatives like rods or algebra tiles aids in their understanding. If that is true of your students, then by all means, keep manipulatives out and ready to use! I find that most manipulatives do not increase understanding or translate to classwork problems for students with dyscalculia. I also find that many manipulatives created for teaching time, money, place value, or fractions are too infantile for older students. No one past third grade wants to be seen using a brightly colored object with a duck or sun printed on it! Use or create age-appropriate manipulatives. Work with your students to determine if the manipulative is creating a change in comprehension or performance. If so, keep using them. If not, move on to the tools that do.

76

Chapter 4 Questions and Exercises

1.   Worked examples give students answers without having them do work. True/False

2.   Middle school math topics are an extension of elementary math topics. True/False

3.   Formulas help all students complete work faster. True/False

4.   Three common math struggles for dyscalculics in middle school are:

   a. Writing graphs, reading graphs, and substitution.
   b. Graphing, problem solving, and working with formulas.
   c. Showing work, following examples, and staying engaged in class.

5.   A schema is best described as:

   a. A blueprint.
   b. A type of problem solving.
   c. A group of related ideas and experiences that lead to actions.

6.   Students with dyscalculia gain a one-half advantage:

   a. Around 7th grade.
   b. Around 4th grade.
   c. Around 10th grade.

7.   Graphing correctly includes:

   a. Using a table of values and graphing calculator.
   b. Following directions.
   c. Visual-spatial skills and recognizing key features.

8.   Reducing errors is useful when:

   a. Raising report card grades.
   b. Strengthening neurological connections.
   c. Completing homework to memorize basic facts.

9. Write a 250-word reflection to the case study. Have you had a similar experience with a student? How would you have approached helping this student?

10. Write a 3-5 page paper describing an intervention lesson to boost one of the following skills: graphing, problem solving, or working with formulas.

Endnotes

[1] Barrett, L. (2021). Your brain predicts (almost) everything you do. *Science*, www.mindful.org. Retrieved October 2022.

[2] Dumontheil, I. (2014). Development of abstract thinking during childhood and adolescence: The role of rostrolateral prefrontal cortex. *Developmental Cognitive Neuroscience, 10*, 57-76.

[3] Haberstroh, S., & Schulte-Körne, G. (2019). The diagnosis and treatment of dyscalculia. *Deutsches Ärzteblatt International, 116*(7), 107.

[4] Kop, P. M., Janssen, F. J., Drijvers, P. H., & van Driel, J. H. (2020). The relation between graphing formulas by hand and students' symbol sense. *Educational Studies in Mathematics, 105*(2), 137-161.

[5] Mazzocco, M. M., Myers, G. F., Lewis, K. E., Hanich, L. B., & Murphy, M. M. (2013). Limited knowledge of fraction representations differentiates middle school students with mathematics learning disability (dyscalculia) versus low mathematics achievement. *Journal of Experimental Child Psychology, 115*(2), 371-387.

[6] Monteiro, C., & Ainley, J. (2003). Developing critical sense in graphing. *Proceedings of III CERME. Available at http://fibonacci. dm. unipi. it/~ didattica/CERME3.*

[7] Peterson, R. L., Boada, R., McGrath, L. M., Willcutt, E. G., Olson, R. K., & Pennington, B. F. (2017). Cognitive prediction of reading, math, and attention: Shared and unique influences. *Journal of Learning Disabilities, 50*(4), 408–421. https://doi.org/10.1177/0022219415618500

[8] Rosselli, M., Matute, E., Pinto, N., & Ardila, A. (2006). Memory abilities in children with subtypes of dyscalculia. *Developmental Neuropsychology, 30*(3), 801-818.

[9] Sweller, J., Van Merrienboer, J. J., & Paas, F. G. (1998). Cognitive architecture and instructional design. *Educational Psychology Review, 10*(3), 251-296.

[10] Wilkey, E. D., Pollack, C., & Price, G. R. (2020). Dyscalculia and typical math achievement are associated with individual differences in number-specific executive function. *Child Development, 91*(2), 596-619.

[11] Young, C. J., Levine, S. C., & Mix, K. S. (2018). The connection between spatial and mathematical ability across development. *Frontiers in Psychology, 9*, 755.

Chapter 5: Dyscalculia in High School

"If you have knowledge, let others light their candles in it."

-- Margaret Fuller

Students with dyscalculia encounter great ironies in high school math classes. The first irony is that all of the math topics which earlier held them back– time, money, place value, multi-digit multiplication and division— disappear. The second irony is that topics repeat– graphing, tables of value, and solving equations– giving them multiple chances to learn and practice what to do. The final irony is that calculators are required and reference sheets are almost always provided. Students are freely given the support they need. It can seem like a daunting task to bring math performance to grade level while also teaching Algebra, Geometry, or Statistics. However, it is easier for secondary students to become successful in math class with less intervention, and this should give teachers hope. High school math topics require fewer numeracy skills; they focus on basic facts under twelve. The four operations– add, subtract, multiply, divide– involve smaller, more familiar digits, rather than the larger, intimidating digits of 4th or 5th grade math (Figure 12). Rarely, if ever, do we carry or borrow.

Figure 12. *High school operations versus elementary operations.*

Elementary math problems	High school math problems
3001 -999	$4x + 5 = 12$ $\underline{-5 \quad -5}$
$\dfrac{3}{7} + \dfrac{2}{3}$	$\dfrac{1}{2}(2x + 4)$
718×25	$-3(m - 3)$

Elementary math classes use longer strings of digits, carrying, borrowing, and larger numbers, while high school math classes use simple operations involving digits under ten.

© EduCalc Learning 2022

We add and subtract fractions during one chapter of Algebra 2, and even then, the bulk of the work is to write factors next to each other instead of jumping to the Least Common Denominator (Figure 13). In fact, if more elementary school students had to write out the factors involved in creating common denominators, they would better understand how to do the same work in Algebra 2! Also, topics repeat throughout high school math classes. We use the same inverse operations when solving equations in Algebra 1, Geometry, and Algebra 2. We graph the same intercepts, slopes, reflections, and other key points on graphs in Algebra 1, Algebra 2, and Calculus. The terms we learn in middle school– range, mean, median, mode, and the odds of an outcome occurring– are the same terms we use, albeit more extensively, in Probability & Statistics. This repetition gives students four years to practice the same set of skills.

Figure 13. *Listing the factors of common denominators.*

$$\frac{3}{5} + \frac{2}{4} \implies \frac{3(4)}{5(4)} + \frac{2(5)}{4(5)}$$

$$\frac{3}{(x+2)} + \frac{2}{(x-1)} \implies \frac{3(x-1)}{(x+2)(x-1)} + \frac{2(x+2)}{(x+2)(x-1)}$$

When elementary school students write out the multiplication of factors that creates common denominators (top row), they are practicing the skills they need to use in higher level math classes (bottom row). © EduCalc Learning 2022

Secondary math teachers should employ six best practices for teaching students with learning disabilities.[4] These instructional strategies are already used by many seasoned, successful educators, but they have an added importance for helping students with issues like dyscalculia. Learning disorders add extra barriers to school success, largely due to the structure and pacing of most K-12 classrooms. Following these best practices removes many structural barriers and helps reinforce learning.[4]

Best Practices for Teaching Students with Disabilities		
Prior achievement	Self-efficacy	Instructional content
Instruction management	Evaluation	Educator beliefs

<u>Prior achievement</u>: Begin lessons by pointing out familiar skills and resources. For students with dyscalculia, this step is a crucial reminder of vocabulary, procedures, and key steps to problem solving. These students usually begin class with a panic response because they do not remember what they learned yesterday or last week. However, giving a prompt can help trigger their memories. Sample prompts include:

> "Today, we're going to talk more about two-step equations. The goal here is to isolate the variable, so first we will look for any constant terms– the numbers by themselves, with no variable– and we will use inverse operations. What's the inverse of adding?"

> "Let's look at some perimeter and area problems that use binomials. For perimeter problems, measuring the length around an object, we're going to add binomials by combining like terms. For area problems, we have to multiply the binomials, so get out your notes for FOILing."

Students without dyscalculia will automatically think of yesterday's work, the notes they wrote down or practice problems they completed, and the processes and procedures involved in a given topic. Students with excellent executive function skills, strong memorization skills, or faster processing speed will recall more information in less time because they have internal structures that activate prior knowledge. Students with dyscalculia do not have the same internal structures that support learning math.[3] For them, trying to remember prior knowledge is a frustrating and confusing experience. Prompting students with dyscalculia is crucial to their engagement in class.

Self-efficacy: Self-efficacy refers to our belief that we can reach goals if we make the effort and use the right resources. Self-efficacy engages and empowers students. In fact, increasing student self-efficacy is directly tied to increased academic performance. Teachers can influence self-efficacy by pointing out a student's strengths. However, the praise has to be genuine or it will not increase self-efficacy (Figure 14).

Figure 14. *Use honest praise.*

Disingenuous Praise	Genuine Praise
"I knew you just needed to try harder."	"I see you verified your answers before turning in your work, that really improved your grade."
"Anybody can do this, it's easy!"	"I see you looked for negative signs before combining terms, and you got more answers right this time."
"You did it yesterday, you can do it today."	"It looks like you changed the way you wrote down your notes, and it seems like that helped you remember what to do."

Students can tell immediately if praise is false and inflated, or sincere. Disingenuous praise can reduce self-esteem and erode the relationship between teacher and student. Genuine praise increases self-esteem, self-confidence, and self-efficacy, while strengthening the bond between student and teacher. © EduCalc Learning 2022

Instructional content: Be direct and clear; use explicit instructions. Help students make connections between warm-up problems and extension problems. Students with dyscalculia will not readily apply their math skills to unfamiliar problems. They need assistance creating both near and far transfer (Figure 15). Teachers can improve transfer by prompting students. Tell them which formula or procedure to use in different situations. Point out the context clues that can trigger using a certain formula or applying a specific concept. This is a common practice when word problems are first introduced; many teachers have students make a booklet or graphic organizer that lists all the words which mean "to add" (add, combine, sum, etc.). Older students can benefit from the same type of organizers in their higher-level math classes.

Figure 15. *Near and far transfer. Near transfer is easier to teach than far transfer, yet students with learning disorders may struggle more with near transfer than their peers. Educators must create a bridge between concepts rather than assuming students will make the leap on their own.*

Math skill	Near transfer	Far transfer
$4 + 6 = 10$	$4 + 6 = 6 + 4$	$2(2 + 3) = 10$
Bananas cost 0.99 cents each and apples cost 0.45 cents each. How much will 5 bananas and 3 apples cost all together?	Jasmine buys 8 pieces of fruit for the week, some 0.99 cent bananas and some 0.45 cent apples. She spends $6.25. How many apples and bananas did she buy?	A fruit salad recipe calls for 1 banana and 0.5 apples per serving. Jasmine wants to bring the salad to a party, but she wants to spend less than $6 on ingredients. If bananas cost 0.99 cents each and apples cost 0.45 cents each, how many servings of fruit salad can Jasmine make?

Near transfer requires using a learned skill in a new, yet familiar, setting. Far transfer requires applying a learned skill to an unfamiliar situation. Students with dyscalculia need educators who can activate prior knowledge of the learned skill and explain how it applies to a new or unusual problem before students attempt to solve problems on their own.
© EduCalc Learning 2022

Instruction management: Are students hearing what you're saying? Are they applying your instructions correctly, or do they seem lost? Managing the pace of instruction and adapting to student progress is important when teaching students with learning disorders. Pay attention to the number of practice problems students need to develop mastery.[4] Students with dyscalculia will need to complete more "beginner" problems before they are ready to move on, partly because teachers do not modify the pace of a lesson.[4] Once students have successfully mastered the foundational skills needed for a given math lesson, they are ready to work independently.

Evaluation: Use a wide variety of assessments to determine a student's strengths and weaknesses. Some students have an easier time writing out their work but aren't sure how to say what they're doing; they need practice using the vocabulary of math. Model how to describe problem solving ("First, I'm going to add 7 to both sides of this equation") and give students the chance to practice explaining their work. Some (especially those with dysgraphia) do a better job of explaining their steps and saying their answers, but have difficulty writing it down. Some students prefer to work with computer-based programs; some prefer to work on paper with plenty of space to show work or doodle. A student who freezes during multiple choice tests may do a fantastic job of creating posters or verbally explaining their work. All of these are acceptable methods of evaluating student understanding of a topic.

Educator beliefs: Too many teachers rely solely on repeating the teaching methods they enjoyed as a student, or using the same strategies they used during their first year of teaching.[4] Keep up with new methods of instruction and take advantage of current research. Remember, there's a reason why doctors no longer use leeches to bleed a patient who has the vapors! The intersection of education, psychology, and neurology have given us an unprecedented understanding of how learning occurs and the ways neuroatypical development impacts learning. Take advantage of professional development opportunities. Read scholarly articles related to your field. Be open to the new discoveries that can radically change your approach, and your students' experiences in your class.

Metacognition, visual-spatial support, and immediate feedback

Metacognition means to think about what we are thinking about. This self-monitoring skill supports students with dyscalculia as they grow into mathematical thinkers. It develops their self-advocacy skills. It can improve their independent work as well. Teachers can help students develop self-monitoring (reflecting on progress) and self-regulation (planning future actions), which supports math mastery.[7] Save time at the end of class to discuss what worked well, what still needs to be improved, and how that improvement might happen. Ask students, "what made sense, and what is still confusing?" then point out how they can support themselves in the future[7]. Simple statements like, "I noticed you followed the steps in the right order, which is great, but combining integers with negative signs gave you trouble. Make a note to double-check those answers before you write them down" give students clear instructions on how to improve.

Visual-spatial issues are common throughout all levels of mathematics.[9] While some students with dyscalculia have low visual-spatial skills, some have above average skills. The only way to know with certainty is to see a full neuropsychological report that lists a visual-spatial percentile rank. However, there may be signs: a student who struggles with writing proofs but can instantly see the correct justification for naming congruent triangles probably has higher visual-spatial skills. A student who uses the correct problem-solving steps in the right order, yet never notices a negative sign or a difference in exponents, probably has lower visual-spatial skills. Teachers can support visual-spatial skills by using color, pointing out key differences, and having students name what they see. This is more than a nice support tool for students with dyscalculia: visual-spatial ability is tied to math achievement, and visual-spatial memory is highly correlated to mathematical abilities.[9] When teachers help strengthen a student's visual-spatial skills, they also increase their chances for mastery in math class.

Finally, the length of time between attempt and feedback must be shortened for students with dyscalculia. They need to know right away what they did right, what they need to correct, and how to make those corrections.[4] Receiving feedback days or weeks after finishing a test is not enough to reinforce understanding. The human brain needs to know right away which actions and behaviors are successful and should be remembered, and which are unsuccessful and should be discarded.[8] This is doubly important for students with dyscalculia, as immediate feedback increases metacognition in students with learning disorders.[6] Students need feedback that is immediate, that mentions specific corrective actions, and that moves them toward their learning objectives.[1]

Case Study 5: William

5th grader William attended the private school where I was a teacher and math specialist. As a young child, William witnessed his parents' bitter divorce and suffered from clinical depression. His school attendance was spotty at best. His attention to schoolwork was limited. He didn't like to be called on, called out, or checked in with by his teachers. He seemed to want to dissolve into the background and be left alone. His schoolwork was below grade level in all subjects, but he seemed to be catching up in English class, science, and social studies. William was not my student, but I was asked to sit in on a parent-teacher conference to discuss what could be done to support him in math class.

It was clear that William suffered from a social-emotional disconnect. Head down, hair over his eyes, slouched in his chair, he rarely made eye contact with anyone and shrugged most of his responses. He never disrupted class, preferring to take out his frustration and anger by shutting down rather than lashing out. William was very behind his peers in math. He didn't ask questions and wouldn't ask for help; his paper would either be blank or full of random guesses. His teachers were frustrated and his parents were out of patience. How could they reach him without sending him farther into his shell?

After listening to the teacher and principal talk about their experiences with William, I suggested they root all of his interactions in social-emotional principles: respect his need for privacy, include him in decision making, and allow him to direct the best path for his learning. It was very important to William that he would not be called out or called on in class. It was equally important to the teacher that she could find out whether or not William understood the lesson. We devised a system of silent communication, using popsicle sticks. William would keep three popsicle sticks on his desk. One would have a red top, one a yellow top, and one a green top. William could put a popsicle stick on his desk to show that understood (green tip), had a question (yellow tip), or felt lost (red tip). The teacher would know to speak with William privately and quietly if he used the yellow or the red tipped stick. William was able to keep his struggles private while also signaling for help. This was a simple fix, but it met his needs and helped him feel safe and respected. William needed this foundation before he could interact with the class or absorb the instruction.

I won't say that William was a brand-new person soon after, because that isn't how progress happens. Recovering from trauma takes time. It can't be predicted or rushed. However, I can say that William began to feel more comfortable in school. He made a few friends and became more talkative with his teachers. This was the first step on a long road to reaching grade level schoolwork. Luckily, his parents made the choice to keep William in his small, private school. He was able to have the same few teachers year after year, including me, and we had the chance to get to know his strengths as a student. We knew what to expect from William and we learned how to adapt our curriculum to his needs.

Years later, William had more friends and a great attitude, but he was still struggling in his classes, so his parents took him to a psychologist for testing. Turns out, William had dyscalculia, dyslexia, and dysgraphia! His learning disabilities were hidden behind his stressful home life and his social-emotional needs. Once we had the proper diagnosis, we were able to ensure that William had the right accommodations, including typing rather than handwriting assignments, using a calculator, and not being graded for spelling and punctuation. Then William was able to truly match his academic potential. Why do some students get tested for learning disabilities late, or never? Sometimes, the delay is due to embarrassment over academic struggles, or ignorance of different learning disabilities, or spending too long in intervention cycles that don't lead anywhere. Sometimes the delay is due to the high cost of testing or a lack of access to qualified professionals. In any case, it's best to know for certain whether a student has a learning disability so that schools and teachers can provide the right kind of help as soon as possible.

Understand, Master, Recall: High School

High school students with dyscalculia struggle with connections: connecting equations to tables of values, connecting equations to graphs, connecting equations to factors, et cetera. While neurotypical students create these connections on their own, teachers must spend more time creating the bridge for neuroatypical students. External connectors like guided notes or worked examples may help. Slowing down instruction until mastery is reached may help. Clearly pointing out the connections may help. Training students in metacognitive reflection may help. Since every student is different, teachers should expect that one approach will not fit all their students with dyscalculia.

Understand.

Whenever possible, teachers should use a CRA (concrete-representation-abstract) method of teaching.[5] In the CRA method, a formula, procedure, or concept is first presented in the most concrete way possible. In algebra, this could mean using a table of values to graph lines, parabolas, and cubic functions before graphing from equations. An example that works in both algebra and geometry involves taking students outside to measure the actual height of people and the length of their shadows, plus the shadow length of trees, cars, or signs. Students would use these real-world measurements to solve for unknown heights. This process can also be applied to finding the missing side of a triangle, solving proportions, proving similar triangles, finding angle measurements using trig functions, and a number of other topics. Once the concrete activity is complete, students can practice solving representational problems on a worksheet or through textbook problems. Finally, the abstract formulas or theorems can be discussed.

Using the strategies presented in this chapter, increasing metacognition, enhancing visual-spatial focus, and giving immediate feedback, are useful tools for times when a CRA model isn't available or practical. They will help students with dyscalculia understand the abstract concepts inherent in high school problem solving. CRA adaptations can be difficult to create– for example, it would be difficult for any teacher to find manipulatives to demonstrate most System of Equations word problems! Also, teachers might be required to follow pacing charts or use a curriculum that does not use CRA strategies. Still, research shows that using CRA whenever possible does lead to increased math performance in other situations.[5] Add in CRA when and where you can.

Master.

Merriam-Webster defines *mastery* as "possession or display of great skill or technique; skill or knowledge that makes one a master of a subject". How can teachers ensure their students with dyscalculia become masters over math? By creating a series of successful events. Students must have successful performances they can reflect on and build from[4]. Continuous success leads to expectations of future success, while continued failure leads to expectations of failure that are difficult to overcome.[4] Educators must notice, amplify, and reproduce successful outcomes for students. This is especially necessary for students with dyscalculia who come to the secondary math class with eight-plus years of failures.

Creating successful events should not be inflated, and it does not have to be difficult. Using scaffolding is an easy way for teachers to increase successful outcomes and improve mastery.[7] Scaffolding allows teaching to be iterative: each event decides and refines the next event. For example, when teaching students with dyscalculia how to find the percent of change, an interventionist or tutor should first show the student how to set up the problem, then explicitly describe each step they use to solve the problem. This pattern is repeated for each percent of change problem: show, describe, solve. Show, describe, solve. Add in some questions for the student: "Now I need to plug some numbers into this proportion. What do you think I should put, and where should it go?" Amplify all successful responses: "Yes, I'll write the x over 100 because that's the part I don't know, and I always want percent over 100, excellent." That successful event is the first step of mastery. Continue solving problems together, letting the student do more of the work on their own, as they are ready. Continue to amplify successful actions: "Yes, x over 100, that's good. Correct, subtract those two. Cross-multiply, nice, and divide, there's your final answer. Good work." Don't hold your confirmation or corrections to the end of the problem. Give students multiple chances to reflect on and correct their work throughout the class.

Recall.

Students with dyscalculia forget math knowledge over time. Many say they can learn a math skill on Monday and have little recollection of the same skill on Thursday. Educators can help students "find" these learned skills by activating prior knowledge.[2] In a typical math class, teachers ask the students questions to activate prior knowledge. This prepares students for class and acts as an informal assessment of retention and recall. However, students with dyscalculia will fail at recall most of the time. For these students, teachers need to reverse the order: tell, don't ask. Remind students of yesterday's vocabulary, formulas, or procedures. Briefly list the problem-solving steps or theorems needed for today's work. Do not expect students with dyscalculia to activate prior knowledge on their own.

What about college? Students with dyscalculia should feel able to apply to any college or university they choose, studying any major they like. Acceptance is based on a number of factors that are out of the scope of this book, but applying or attending college should not seem out of reach because of dyscalculia. There are a growing number of colleges that are test-optional, and some schools are designed specifically for students with SLDs. students should practice advocacy skills and talk to their colleges of choice about which accommodations are available. As for any student, the most important part of going to college is finding the school that is the best fit for the student and their learning needs.

Chapter 5 Questions and Exercises

1. Students with dyscalculia need a new set of teaching strategies. True/False

2. Feedback is helpful whenever it is given. True/False

3. Dyscalculia is worse in secondary math classes. True/False

4. Three useful strategies for teaching students with dyscalculia include:

    a. Assessing prior knowledge, self-efficacy, and changing teacher beliefs.

    b. Extra practice, mastering prior math topics, and memorization.

    c. Practicing standardized tests, learning basic facts, and using computers.

5. Scaffolding is a method of teaching that:

    a. Can increase mastery by creating successful events.

    b. Is appropriate for elementary students but not older students.

    c. Has been proven to be ineffective.

6. Teacher-to-student feedback should be:

    a. Positive all the time.

    b. Immediate and authentic.

    c. Given after tests and projects or when asked for.

7. Near and far transfer can be described as:

    a. A way to measure student study habits.

    b. An indication that a student can work independently.

    c. Applying knowledge to new and unfamiliar situations.

8. Three best practices for teaching students with learning differences are:

    1. Using modified curriculum, alternative assessments, and low expectations.

    2. Instructional content, instruction management, and teacher beliefs.

    3. Separate instruction areas, modified textbooks, and no tests.

9. Write a 250-word reflection to the case study. Have you had a similar experience with a student? How would you have approached helping this student?

10. Write a 3-5 page paper describing how to use CRA in a math unit.

Endnotes

[1] Chang, N. (2011). Pre-service teachers' views: How did E-feedback through assessment facilitate their learning? *Journal of the Scholarship of Teaching and Learning*, 16-33.

[2] Elbro, C., & Buch-Iversen, I. (2013). Activation of background knowledge for inference making: Effects on reading comprehension. *Scientific studies of reading*, *17*(6), 435-452.

[3] Geary, D. C. (2011). Consequences, characteristics, and causes of mathematical learning disabilities and persistent low achievement in mathematics. *Journal of Developmental & Behavioral Pediatrics*, *32*(3), 250-263.

[4] Jones, E. D., Wilson, R., & Bhojwani, S. (1997). Mathematics instruction for secondary students with learning disabilities. *Journal of learning disabilities*, *30*(2), 151-163.

[5] Myers, J. A., Wang, J., Brownell, M. T., & Gagnon, J. C. (2015). Mathematics interventions for students with learning disabilities (LD) in secondary school: A review of the literature. *Learning Disabilities: A Contemporary Journal*, *13*(2), 207-235.

[6] Roll, I., Aleven, V., McLaren, B. M., & Koedinger, K. R. (2011). Improving students' help-seeking skills using metacognitive feedback in an intelligent tutoring system. *Learning and instruction*, *21*(2), 267-280.

[7] Schneider, W., & Artelt, C. (2010). Metacognition and mathematics education. *ZDM*, *42*(2), 149-161.

[8] Sheneman, L., Schossau, J., & Hintze, A. (2019). The evolution of neuroplasticity and the effect on integrated information. *Entropy*, *21*(5), 524.

[9] Woolner, P. (2004). A comparison of a visual-spatial approach and a verbal approach to teaching mathematics. *International Group for the Psychology of Mathematics Education*.

Chapter 6: Conclusion

"If everyone is thinking alike, then somebody isn't thinking."

-- George S. Patton

As soon as people develop motor control, we pick things up. We group things together in piles. We move objects from here to there. Our understanding of quantity comes from *doing* something. Even in the most rudimentary cultures around the world, humans develop an understanding of one, two, and three objects. Amounts greater than three are simply *many* or *more*. This understanding of quantity comes from interacting with the environment. For children with typical neurodevelopment, these external experiences create internal structures that support numeracy– the Approximate Number System that drives estimating, cardinality, ordinality, and pattern recognition. Children with dyscalculia have atypical neurodevelopment, and they require external support for longer periods of time.

However, extended support does not have to mean delayed academic success. When students use the right accommodation for their needs, they can progress quickly. For example, once they have consistently used a calculator to verify calculations, they may use it to double check their work before handing in classwork, but they've gotten most of the answers right the first time. They may want to review their notes before starting class, because activating prior knowledge is difficult for them, but they recall information more quickly. Once they've learned time management strategies, they make better use of extended time for tests and projects. After experiencing repeated moments of success, they have better self-confidence, more self-efficacy, and they are willing to take on the challenge of learning new math topics because they believe they can be successful.

Teaching students with dyscalculia

Teaching students with dyscalculia requires different work, but not more work, by teachers. It requires understanding atypical neurological development and the challenges it creates. First, the Approximate Number Sense (ANS) develops slowly and with less strength than in typical neurodevelopment. Second, mathematical knowledge is learned and then forgotten as the parietal lobe loses math information over time. Third, the steps, procedures, and formulas that guide most students do not support neuroatypical students; they act as barriers instead. These academic challenges will not be overcome through extra practice. Students with dyscalculia require accommodations that provide external support as they work. These include having a times tables list or a calculator, having worked examples or guided notes, or having reference sheets showing formulas or values of coins. Students without dyscalculia are using the exact same support systems, but theirs are internal. Their ANS, properly stored memories, and strong recall of mathematical information are giving them instant support which simply does not exist in the same way for students with dyscalculia.

Students with dyscalculia are perfectly capable of mastering math concepts, succeeding in higher-level math classes, and pursuing math careers, although they may not believe it. The first step to changing the negative beliefs that hold these students back is to help students demonstrate their abilities; the second step is to build on their successes. The job of the dyscalculia-trained educator is two-fold: knowing how to reach, teach, and support students with dyscalculia, and knowing how to increase self-confidence and self-efficacy within their students. We can do this through scaffolding, using metacognition strategies, and allowing students to use the right support tools for the topic at hand.

Teachers may feel frustrated as they repeatedly teach the same topic over and over without seeing the same results as in their non-dyscalculic students. When we understand why students with dyscalculia struggle to retain or recall math knowledge, that frustration lessens. Educators might have to change their idea of what a "good" math student looks like. Let go of the ideal mental math master with perfect memorization. Instead, reach students through games, puzzles, or art activities that give them access to the world of math. Support those with dyscalculia by using appropriate external support tools, like a times tables list, a reference sheet with worked examples, or using a calculator. Expect students to immediately check their work and confirm their answers. Require precision and accuracy rather than memorization. Soon you will see the results you are looking for.

It can be difficult to change our beliefs about teaching and learning. The conversations around learning differences, neurodivergent students, and the importance of self-beliefs are new and, for some, uncomfortable. Yet, they are necessary. They are correct. And they produce results. Too frequently, the biggest barrier to academic achievement is the classroom itself, but as teachers, we have the power to create and to change student experiences through our choice of instruction, our use of interventions, and our acceptance of accommodations.

Finding new ways to teach differently developing children is not a new concept. The first public school in America, the Boston Latin School, opened in 1635; the desire to provide a free and equitable education for all children soon became a founding principle of the United States. The first school for the deaf, The American Asylum in Hartford, Connecticut, opened in 1821. Perkins School for the Blind opened in Massachusetts in 1829. The Cotting School for children with physical disabilities opened in Massachusetts in 1893. The Gow School for students with dyslexia opened in 1926 in New York. Modern public schools meet the needs of students with a wide range of learning challenges, all across the country. We do better when we know better. Today, we know more about dyscalculia than ever before. It is time we do better.

Case Study 6: Jonathan

Jonathan was in 9th grade when he was finally diagnosed with dyscalculia. Before that, he had experienced years of struggling, trying, and failing math classes. These failures were tough for Jonathan to accept because he enjoyed school, was a bright child, and was able to succeed in all other subjects. Discovering that there was an identifiable reason for his persistent math issues was a relief– there was a name and a condition that could finally be addressed. His parents and his teachers had never heard of dyscalculia. The school wasn't sure what they could do to help Jonathan. Local tutors were also unfamiliar with this learning disorder. Jonathan's mom found me through a social media support group and we began tutoring during the second 9 weeks of his Algebra 1 class.

The first thing I asked was that Jonathan had the exact same calculator at home as the one he would use in school. Students almost never have the same calculator in both places, and it is critical that they use one machine, all the time, as they build confidence and understanding. Instead, what typically happens is that students are allowed to use a graphing calculator at school, they use their phone calculator at home, and they have lost the calculator that was purchased over the summer or handed down by an older sibling. Most of their homework time is spent learning how to use or find a certain calculator function, or completing work while incorrectly marking the negative sign or root symbol, which leads to wrong answers. They do not develop an understanding of their math work.

Jonathan was a very conscientious student. He always had his homework and class notebook with him. He knew the dates of his upcoming quizzes and tests. He wrote down as many notes in class as he could, whether or not he understood what they meant (that was our job in tutoring, to make sense of what he heard in class). I could tell he had great executive function and working memory skills. What he didn't have was the basic facts memorized, or the ability to consistently remember the steps to follow when solving a problem. Stopping to think about these things slowed him down to where he couldn't keep up with the class or the teacher's instructional pace. He struggled to develop automaticity since he was repeatedly questioning himself and his work.

During our first few sessions, I would remind Jonathan to "put it in the calculator and tell me what you get", before he guessed at answers. I also used prompts like, "tell me the formula for this again", or "do you still have the page with the steps written down? Read me those steps, let's make sure we've got them all". Over time, these reminders helped him build strong work habits: verifying the formula, reviewing the steps, confirming the answers. The more he used these habits, the more answers he got right. The more times he was right, the faster he became at completing problems. The faster he became at his work, the more confidence he developed in his abilities. Soon, he was explaining topics to me, and our time was spent finessing his work: discussing test-taking strategies, determining how he could best take notes so he understood them later, reviewing his study plans or timelines to complete larger projects.

By the end of the first semester, Jonathan's Algebra 1 grade had risen from a low F to a mid-C. By the end of the third 9 weeks, he had an A in class. The following year, Jonathan took Geometry. We started the year with weekly tutoring sessions where we discussed the conceptual goals of Geometry as opposed to the problem-solving goals of Algebra. We discussed the pacing, format, and expectations of this new teacher and planned how Jonathan could be successful in this class. We talked about how he could explain his learning challenges to his teacher, and how to ask good questions in class. Soon we tapered off our sessions to an as-needed basis. Jonathan continued getting A's by using his work habits, resources, and self-advocacy to support himself.

Chapter 1 Answer Key

1. People with dyscalculia can get better at math with extra practice. True/**False**

2. Many people struggle with math because they aren't good students. True/**False**

3. Dyscalculia affects 8-12% of the population. **True**/False

4. Three key indicators of dyscalculia include:
   a. Low math scores, poor learning attitude, and working speed.
   b. **Trouble telling time and working with money, and forgetting math facts**.
   c. Speed, study skills, and telling time.

5. The four stages of early math development are:
   a. **Cardinality, comparison, problem solving, and measurement.**
   b. Skip counting, comparison, shape sorting, and measurement.
   c. Cardinality, counting principles, problem solving, and work ethic.

6. Where does dyscalculia come from?
   a. Genetics.
   b. Brain injuries.
   c. **Both are possible**.

7. Which of the following are Specific Learning Disorders?
   a. Dyslexia, ADHD, ELL.
   b. **Dyscalculia, dyslexia, dysgraphia**.
   c. Any learning challenge.

8. What is subitization?
   a. **Automatically estimating amounts**.
   b. A form of subtraction.
   c. A type of math instruction.

Chapter 2 Answer Key

1. Children develop mathematical thinking over many years. **True**/False

2. Practicing math on worksheets strengthens the ANS in young children. True/**False**

3. Children with dyscalculia struggle to develop automaticity when counting. **True**/False

4. The five stages of mathematical thinking are:
   a. Emerging, practicing, mastering, showing, and teaching.
   b. Concrete, abstract, manipulative, figurative, and written.
   c. **Emergent, perceptual, figurative, initial, and facile.**

5. Subitization helps people:
   a. **Mentally estimate and compare amounts.**
   b. Subtract math problems.
   c. Substitute values in math problems.

6. The Approximate Number System (ANS) includes:
   a. Subitization
   b. Cardinality
   c. **Both are part of ANS**

7. Coding math concepts includes:
   a. **Matching quantity, words, and images in our heads.**
   b. Matching two or more ideas in our head.
   c. The cardinality and ordinality of numbers.

8. Working memory:
   a. Is something everyone has in equal amounts.
   b. **Is negatively impacted by stress, but can predict later math achievements.**
   c. Develops naturally over time and has little impact on learning.

Chapter 3 Answer Key

1. Having a list of steps or procedures gives some students an unfair advantage over their peers. True/**False**

2. Mentally rotating objects begins with physically rotating objects. **True**/False

3. Signs of dyscalculia usually appear later, after 5th grade. True/**False**

4. Three common math struggles for dyscalculics in early elementary are:
   a. Writing numbers backwards, telling time, and numbers in word form.
   b. **Telling time, working with money, and place value.**
   c. Completing work, writing numbers backward, and counting to 5.

5. Finger counting after second grade is:
   a. **A potential sign of a learning disability.**
   b. An example of lazy work.
   c. A crutch that should be discouraged.

6. Students should do grade level work:
   a. After they have mastered the foundations of earlier work.
   b. When they are ready to do the work independent of support tools.
   c. **At all times**.

7. Forgetting steps and procedures is:
   a. A sign that the student did not study.
   b. **Common among people with dyscalculia.**
   c. A barrier that cannot be overcome.

8. Place value was developed:
   a. By mathematicians in Babylonia in the 12th century.
   b. **By a mathematician in India in the 5th century.**
   c. By Renaissance mathematicians in Italy.

Chapter 4 Answer Key

1. Worked examples give students answers without having them do work. True/**False**

2. Middle school math topics are an extension of elementary math topics. True/**False**

3. Formulas help all students complete work faster. True/**False**

4. Three common math struggles for dyscalculics in middle school are:
   a. Writing graphs, reading graphs, and substitution.
   b. **Graphing, problem solving, and working with formulas.**
   c. Showing work, following examples, and staying engaged in class.

5. A schema is best described as:
   a. A blueprint.
   b. A type of problem solving.
   c. **A group of related ideas and experiences that lead to actions**.

6. Students with dyscalculia gain a one-half advantage:
   a. **Around 7th grade.**
   b. Around 4th grade.
   c. Around 10th grade.

7. Graphing correctly includes:
   a. Using a table of values and graphing calculator.
   b. Following directions.
   c. **Visual-spatial skills and recognizing key features**.

8. Reducing errors is useful when:
   a. Raising report card grades.
   b. **Strengthening neurological connections.**
   c. Completing homework to memorize basic facts.

Chapter 5 Answer Key

1. Students with dyscalculia need a new set of teaching strategies. True/**False**

2. Feedback is helpful whenever it is given. True/**False**

3. Dyscalculia is worse in secondary math classes. True/**False**

4. Three useful strategies for teaching students with dyscalculia include:

    a. **Assessing prior knowledge, self-efficacy, and changing teacher beliefs.**

    b. Extra practice, mastering prior math topics, and memorization.

    c. Practicing standardized tests, learning basic facts, and using computers.

5. Scaffolding is a method of teaching that:

    a. **Can increase mastery by creating successful events.**

    b. Is appropriate for elementary students but not older students.

    c. Has been proven to be ineffective.

6. Teacher-to-student feedback should be:

    a. Positive all the time.

    b. **Immediate and authentic.**

    c. Given after tests and projects or when asked for.

7. Near and far transfer can be described as:

    a. A way to measure student study habits.

    b. An indication that a student can work independently.

    c. **Applying knowledge to new and unfamiliar situations.**

8. Three best practices for teaching students with learning differences are:

    a. Using modified curriculum, alternative assessments, and low expectations.

    b. **Instructional content, instruction management, and teacher beliefs.**

    c. Separate instruction areas, modified textbooks, and no tests.

Additional resources

Ashcraft, M. H., & Kirk, E. P. (2001). The relationship among working memory, math anxiety and performance. *Journal of Experimental Psychol*ogy 130, 224–237.

Butterworth, B., Varma, S., & Laurillard, D. (2011). Dyscalculia: From brain to education. *Science, 332*(6033), 1049-1053.

Gibbs, A. S., Hinton, V. M., & Flores, M. M. (2018). A case study using CRA to teach students with disabilities to count using flexible numbers: Applying skip counting to multiplication. *Preventing School Failure: Alternative Education for Children and Youth, 62*(1), 49-57.

Grabner, R. H., Ansari, D., Reishofer, G., Stern, E., Ebner, F., & Neuper, C. (2007). Individual differences in mathematical competence predict parietal brain activation during mental calculation. *Neuroimage, 38*(2), 346-356.

He, Y., Zhou, X., Shi, D., Song, H., Zhang, H., & Shi, J. (2016). New evidence on causal relationship between Approximate Number System (ANS) acuity and arithmetic ability in elementary-school students: A longitudinal cross-lagged Analysis. *Frontiers in psychology, 7*, 1052. https://doi.org/10.3389/fpsyg.2016.01052

Howell, K., & Morehead, M. K. (1987). *Curriculum-based evaluation for special and remedial education: A handbook for deciding what to teach*. Merrill.

Jensen, E. (2008). *Enriching the brain: How to maximize every learner's potential*. Jossey-Bass.

Kaufmann, L., Mazzocco, M. M., Dowker, A., von Aster, M., Goebel, S., Grabner, R., & Rubinsten, O. (2013). Dyscalculia from a developmental and differential perspective. *Frontiers in Psychology, 4*, 516.

Kaufmann, L., & von Aster, M. (2012). The diagnosis and management of dyscalculia. *Deutsches Ärzteblatt International*, 109(45), 767.

Kerry, L. & Swee, Ng (2011). Neuroscience and the teaching of mathematics. *Educational Philosophy and Theory, 86*(43). Doi 10.1111/j.1469-5812.2010.00711.x

Mammarella, I. C., Caviola, S., Giofrè, D., & Szűcs, D. (2018). The underlying structure of visuospatial working memory in children with mathematical learning disability. *British Journal of Developmental Psychology, 36*(2), 220-235.

Mazzocco, M. M., & Thompson, R. E. (2005). Kindergarten predictors of math learning disability. *Learning Disabilities Research & Practice, 20*(3), 142-155.

Munn, P., & Reason, R. (1978). Arithmetical difficulties: Developmental and instructional perspectives. *Arithmetical Difficulties: Developmental and Instructional Perspectives, 24*(2), 5.

Null, J. W. (2017). *Curriculum: From theory to practice.* Rowman & Littlefield.

Piazza, M., Facoetti, A., Trussardi, A. N., Berteletti, I., Conte, S., Lucangeli, D., et al. (2010). Developmental trajectory of number acuity reveals a severe impairment in developmental dyscalculia. *Cognition* 116, 33–41. doi: 10.1016/j.cognition.2010.03.012

Poland, M., & van Oers, B. (2007). Effects of schematising on mathematical development. *European Early Childhood Education Research Journal, 15*(2), 269-293.

Price, G. R., & Ansari, D. (2013). Dyscalculia: Characteristics, causes, and treatments. *Numeracy, 6*(1), 1-16.

Shalev, R. S., & Gross-Tsur, V. (2001). Developmental dyscalculia. *Pediatric neurology, 24*(5), 337-342.

Zadina, J. N. (2014). *Multiple pathways to the student brain: Energizing and enhancing instruction.* Jossey-Bass.

The Author

Dr. Honora Wall, Ed.D., is an educator, author, speaker, and dyscalculia specialist. She studies the impact of atypical neurodevelopment on learning, with a focus on dyscalculia, attention deficit hyperactivity disorder, executive function issues, and processing speed issues. She trains teachers to identify and address barriers to learning in the classroom so students can be successful in any setting. Dr. Wall combines research and classroom-tested strategies to help students across the U.S. reach and exceed grade level math proficiency. Her teacher training courses can be found at educalclearning.com.

Other titles by Honora Wall

Ah-Ha! Games for the Brain

Alignment Teaching: A Journal for Educators

My College Planner

The Story of Me: Advisory Curriculum